11-7-14

Brian & Linda:

Thanks for your interest
in Newberg's history.

George Edmonston

NEWBERG
STORIES FROM
THE GRUBBY END

GEORGE P. EDMONSTON JR.

THE OREGON PRESS

For Lucy Limb Edmonston
and her love for Yamhill County

NEWBERG

STORIES FROM

THE GRUBBY END

Table of Contents

Acknowledgements

First, I want to thank Gary Allen, managing editor of the *Newberg Graphic*, for asking me to do the column in his newspaper that produced the stories in this book. I am also especially indebted to Denise Reilly of the Newberg Public Library and Leah Griffith, director of the library, for all the support they have given over the years in helping me and many others research the history of Newberg and Yamhill County. I also want to thank the following men and women for graciously sharing both their knowledge of and love for Newberg's past: Newberg Mayor Bob Andrews; A-dec co-founders Ken and Joan Austin; George Fox University historian Dr. Ralph Beebe; retired Newberg Fire Chief Al Blodgett; GFU archivist Zoie Clark; Sam Farmer, retired GFU vice president; Cameo Theater owner Brian Francis; Darrol Hockett, retired sexton of the Newberg Friends Cemetery; Geary Linhart, president of the Newberg Historical Society from 2011-2014; retired math teacher Verne Martin; Sarah Munro, director of the Hoover-Minthorn House Museum; John Newman of the Newberg Historical Society; Marjorie Owens, research librarian for the Yamhill County Historical Society; Mike Ragsdale, director of the Newberg Downtown Coalition; and Clyde Thomas, GFU director of plant services. ❖

"They came to this neck of the woods
when it was dubbed the 'grubby end' of Yamhill county
on account of the uninviting conditions that then existed here.
There was not a church building or a schoolhouse worthy
of the name within a radius of eight to fifteen miles
in any direction from the present site of Newberg."

Ezra H. Woodward
Editor and Publisher
Newberg Graphic
Nov. 26, 1908

"It is a difficult problem to select the most interesting incident that occurred
in the development of Newberg and the territory surrounding, over a period of
58 years of my contact with East Chehalem valley, or, what was at one time
called the 'Grubby End' of Chehalem valley."

C.J. Edwards
Son of legendary Newberg Quaker Jesse Edwards
Newberg Graphic
April 1939

"From the 'grubby acres' that characterized early-day Newberg the families
that came here subdued the area. Nearby, the pioneers cut the forest, broke
the land, stumped it, organized it, built on it, made its roadways."

Newberg Graphic
Silver Anniversary Edition
1963

Introduction

One hundred years ago, folks living around Newberg referred to this section of Yamhill County as the "Grubby End," maybe because famers felt the soil wasn't as good for wheat or row crops as, say, over around Lafayette or McMinnville or across the Willamette River in French Prairie.

At least that was the perception.

The fact that Newberg was the last major settlement in the north Willamette Valley to incorporate (the year was 1889) seemed to bear this out. The towns of Lafayette and Yamhill incorporated in 1843. Amity dates to 1849, Dayton to 1850, McMinnville to 1876, Sheridan to 1880.

But the perception was wrong.

By the turn of the century, the "Grubby End" had become a badge of honor, sustained by the knowledge that Newberg settlers had taken a piece of ground many thought was second-rate, found that it was ideal for grasslands and orchard crops, and used this knowledge to develop one of Oregon's most dynamic small cities, with a portfolio of history and achievement unrivaled by any community of the same size in the Pacific Northwest.

Native Americans thrived here for centuries. Later, the Indo-European settlement of Oregon had an early start with the construction of the Willamette Post just south of Newberg around the time of the War of 1812.

In the 1820s, the town of Champoeg appeared just a few miles upriver from Newberg and in 1834 Ewing Young's chose the West Chehalem Valley four miles from Newberg to build his cabin and a nearby grist mill. In 1843, several pioneers from the Great Migration Wagon Train chose this location to begin their Yamhill County odyssey.

In the 1870s, Newberg became the center of Quakerism in the western United States. In the 1880s, a young Quaker lad named Herbert Hoover moved here, grew up here under the guidance of an aunt and uncle who were his foster parents, then went on to become the 31st president of the United States.

Today, Newberg is home to one of the world's largest manufacturers of dental equipment and is at the gateway of a world-famous wine industry.

In 2011 the *Newberg Graphic* asked me to celebrate Newberg's historic past by writing a column telling these and many other stories from east Yamhill County.

I called it "Tales from the Grubby End." This book, *Newberg: Stories from the Grubby End* represents a collection of some of my favorite features from this column and my hope is that you enjoy reading them as much as I have enjoyed writing them.

It was never my intention for this compilation to be a comprehensive history of Newberg and so the reader will not find stories in these pages about Joseph Rogers, who platted the first town in the area near the present Willamette River landing that bears his name and which he called "Chehalem"; or Sebastian Brutscher, who gave us the name Newberg after being inspired to do so from the spelling of his hometown Newburgh in his native country of Bavaria; or even David and Susan Ramsey, whose grist mill and house located on the banks of the Chehalem Creek south and east of town are among the first dwellings in this area and whose presence inspired others to build here as well.

These and other important local personalities have been covered a lot over the past century and the interested reader will have no trouble finding historians who have done a terrific job paying these early pioneers the rich tributes they deserve.

Clearly, these omissions leave me vulnerable to criticism by readers who know Newberg far better than I do and so let me apologize now to anyone who finds missing in these pages a favorite name, date, event or family member.

Where exactly was the "Grubby End?" As best I can tell, there was never any one location for the moniker but a combination of places all in the easternmost section of the county, including Newberg, Dundee, Springbrook and possibly even out Highway 240 on the road toward Carlton and Yamhill.

Or maybe the "Grubby End" was never more than a state of mind.

If you've read some, most or all of these stories from past issues of the *Graphic*, do you need to buy this book?

I'll leave the answer up to you.

However, as you decide, please keep in mind the versions presented here differ in some cases from how they appear in the *Graphic* and reflect the work I've done recently to update facts and correct mistakes.

In most cases, the headlines also differ and the stories have been grouped into categories based on time period and subject matter.

I've dedicated this book to my wife, Lucy Limb Edmonston, for her unbending love for Oregon and Yamhill County and for showing me how special Newberg really is. ❖

George Edmonston Jr.
August 16, 2014

A quartet of historians

Many have asked where I get my ideas for stories.

Back issues of the *Newberg Graphic* provide loads of grist. Readers also offer important input.

In addition, there are four other major sources I hold in very high esteem. The treasures these historians provide are so important no serious research into the local past is complete without some knowledge of their work.

In alphabetical order, say hello to Doris Huffman, Jennie Miller, Ruth Stoller and Minnie Van Valin.

Doris A. Jones Huffman was born on Jan. 10, 1922, to Emery and Elva Parrish Jones and was a sixth-generation Oregonian. She was proud of the fact that she was descended from ancestors who came to Newberg on the Oregon Trail in 1849, and from England via the sea route in 1853.

A major contributor of history features to the *Graphic* (see *A Century to Remember: Newberg 1889-1989*), Huffman also wrote *Oregon's Flamboyant Fourth: 1876* (self-published in 1976).

It offers the story, county-by-county, of Oregon's celebration of the Centennial of the United States. In 1977 it won a national merit award from the American Association for State and Local History.

Her pamphlet, "The Everests: A Family History of Yamhill County," is a treasure of "Grubby End" history. Anyone interested in early clubs, music, organizations, schools, newspapers, Chehalem Valley post offices, and how Newberg got its name would be wise to look here.

Tragically, Huffman was killed in a traffic accident on Rex Hill, Sept. 15, 1997. Her husband, Donald Huffman, had lost his life in an automobile accident several years prior.

Jennie D. Miller was the Newberg City Librarian for 25 years, 1920-1945.

Her manuscript, *A History of Newberg: 1936-1937-1938*, remains the most in-depth study of this city ever done.

Copies of this typewritten document are rare, but make no mistake about it, Miller's *History* is considered a must-read for anyone wanting a better understanding of what life was like in Newberg during the years before World War II.

A resident of Newberg for 60 years and heavily involved in the fraternal and civic activities of this community for over five decades, she was 93 years old when she passed away in 1957. The house she built at 801 E. Sheridan Street still stands.

Miller was a native of Bucksport, Maine. She relocated to Oregon with her parents when she was in her early teens.

In the mid-1930s she began collecting materials pertaining to Newberg's history, including newspaper clippings, old records, private interviews and other sources of institutional memory.

Her legacy continues at our library today in the growing amount of space devoted to the collection and preservation of Newberg's past.

Ruth Annette Cramer Stoller was born Oct. 26, 1915 in Portland. She grew up in Newberg, attended Rex Grade School and Newberg High and graduated from Willamette University in 1942.

She married Harvey Stoller in 1945 and moved to the Dayton area. There, she spent the next 48 years farming, raising five children, and preserving Yamhill County's past.

She devoted decades to researching local pioneers and was always willing to help others search for information on their respective families.

Stoller studied, cataloged and wrote about hundreds of topics on state and county history. Newberg was a personal favorite.

Her volunteer work for the Yamhill County Historical Society spanned many years. Today, the YCHS's research library at the Miller Log Museum on Market Street in Lafayette is named for her.

Among her many publications, the one that has been most valuable to me is titled *Old Yamhill: The Early History of Its Towns and Cities*, first published by Binford & Mort of Portland in 1976. She also authored *From Yamhill to Tillamook by Stagecoach* and *Schools of Old Yamhill*.

She passed away at age 78 in May 1994.

A noted genealogist in the Pacific Northwest, **Minnie Olivia Davis Van Valin** authored at least 38 manuscripts tracing the histories of early Oregon families. In 1953 she co-authored the highly respected *Pioneer Families of Yamhill County*.

She died with her husband, a prominent Newberg dentist, in a Colorado plane crash in 1955. ❖

EARLY
SETTLERS

Who came first? Kalapuyas, French, Quakers, English?

In 2010, on a highway holiday back to Newberg from New Orleans, Lucy and I decided somewhere around Dallas, Texas, to do what we had talked about for years.

We pointed our Ford Explorer north to Grand Island, Neb. This would be our entry point to the 1,800-mile trip west known as the Auto Tour Route of the Oregon National Historic Trail.

Roughly speaking, the route follows the Oregon Trail all the way to Oregon City using I-80, U.S. 30 and I-84. Through the comforts of modern transportation, and assisted by a wonderful device known as cruise control, we would see the "road" the pioneers walked to make the trip here to the Willamette Valley.

Two words: *long* walk.

We had Billy with us, our Chocolate Lab, and a man named Joseph Hess.

Billy, of course, is real. As I write this column, he's nearby, using hungry eyes to beg for lunch.

Mr. Hess was only a figure in my imagination. To the best I have been able to determine, he and his wife Mary were the first Oregon Trail family to settle here at the "Grubby End." Hess Creek? You get the point.

They came with the "Great Migration Wagon Train of 1843," the first train to prove wagons with families could travel west past Fort Hall, Idaho, and make it to Oregon.

God rest their souls, these former residents who came from the good state of Arkansas have been deceased a long time.

Before the arrival of pioneers to the Chehalem Valley, the area had been inhabited by Native American bands collectively known as the Kalapuyas. Across the river, the location that was Champoeg had been a Kalapuya gathering place for generations.

Along the banks of Chehalem Creek, a Kalapuya band known as the Yamhelas, or Yam-els, appear to have occupied a village called Cham-ho-huo. From them we get the name "Yamhill."

A second phase occurred with the establishment of the Willamette Post in 1813. Its owners were from Montreal, Canada. For 20 years this was an important staging area for the fur trade going on as far south as California. To see the actual ground, cross the Willamette River on Hwy 219, go two-tenths of a mile past the bridge and look for a big wooden marker on the left. Stop and read the story.

Next came the settlement of Champoeg itself, a full-blown pioneer village by the late 1830s. Before it was Champoeg, it was known to trappers as Sand's Encampment or Sand Point.

The fourth phase started with a Tennessean named Ewing Young. It included his partners and friends and their considerable activity about four miles west (on Hwy 240 to Carlton/Yamhill) of present-day Newberg in the Chehalem Valley.

Young's dates as a local begin in 1834 and conclude with his death in 1841. His neighbor was Sidney Smith, a member of the ill-fated Peoria Party of 1839, who settled near Young in early September of that year.

A fifth phase was represented by a small group of retired French Canadian trappers who were joined shortly after by American and European farmers using the Oregon Trail to relocate to the north Willamette Valley. This latter group came from many places, but especially England, Scotland, the states of North Carolina, Tennessee and Arkansas, and from states in the Midwest.

About the French, local historian Ruth Stoller discovered that Hudson's Bay Company (HBC) fur trappers knew this location as "Wild Horse Prairie." It seems that both sides of the river were involved.

As the southern brigades would make their way north to refurbish themselves and their supplies on the Columbia River at Fort Vancouver, headquarters of the HBC, this is where they would leave their horses to graze.

Returning south to begin fall trapping, the horses were usually wild from several months roaming the lush grass lands of French Prairie; thus the name. Close to Newberg, Parrett Mountain was known as "Wild Horse Mountain."

With a built-in fondness for the area, many of these men returned to establish their homesteads. Although the numbers settling near Newberg were never anything like that which occurred between Champoeg, St. Paul, and down to Salem, the trappers who did venture to the "Grubby End," combined with a scattering of Oregon Trail pioneers from the earliest wagon trains, represent the first non-native settlers to live in and around what would one day be Newberg.

The final phase was defined by the noticeable influx of members of the Society of Friends, or Quakers, who came to Newberg under the spiritual guidance of William Hobson in the 1870s.

It is also important to note that distinctions exist between these phases as to the long-term impact each would have in Newberg's development as more than just a scattering of farms.

Thus: Members of the Willamette Post, in the main, either left the area or landed elsewhere in the vicinity of French Prairie.

Thus: With the rare exceptions we have already discussed, most of those who came here in the 1830s were also flow-through visitors.

In phase five we finally see enough homesteaders of the more permanent variety to give our town its opening spark.

And it would be the Quakers in the 1870s and '80s who would finally make it happen. ❖

The Willamette Post

Two hundred years ago, the North West Company, a Canadian outfit, founded a small fur trade facility three miles south of Newberg known as the Willamette Post. It was located less than a quarter mile from the south shore of the Willamette River.

To see the former site, cross the Hwy 219 bridge toward St. Paul and look for a large historical marker beside the road.

Only three Euro-American settlements in the Pacific Northwest are older: Fort Astoria (established March 1811) near the mouth of the Columbia River; Fort Okanogan (September 1811), located on the upper Columbia in the state of Washington between the towns of Brewster and Bridgeport; and the Wallace House (c. 1812) near Salem.

The Willamette Post was a going concern, with some periods of inactivity, until the early days of the town of Champoeg in the 1830s.

If Newberg had nothing more than the Willamette Post—no Hoover-Minthorn House, no A-dec, no George Fox University, no wine industry, no Quakers—this tiny pioneer settlement would be enough to put us on the map and keep us there.

The nascent beginnings for the post are somewhat complicated so here's my attempt to piece together what happened.

The idea for such a facility (to help trappers sell their beaver pelts in exchange for supplies for the next hunt) happened a year earlier on the east bank of the Willamette several miles north of Salem. This was the aforementioned Wallace House.

It was built by a group of employees of the Pacific Fur Company, a North West rival. Pacific was owned by America's first millionaire, John Jacob Astor(1763-1848). The construction and operation of the house came under the direction of company clerks William Wallace and J.C. Halsey.

Pacific Fur also owned forts Astoria and Okanogan.

Astor's Pacific Fur, out of concern its investments would be lost to the strong British presence in the Pacific Northwest during the War of 1812, sold both of these forts to the British-owned North West Company on Oct. 16, 1813.

The new owners, headquartered in Montreal, Canada, immediately changed the name of Fort Astoria to the more British-sounding Fort George. They kept Okanogan open, phased out the Wallace facility (closed by 1814) and began construction of a replacement, our very own Willamette Post.

Under the charge of North West clerk William Henry, it was built sometime around December 1813. Constructed were a dwelling house for company employees and two huts for Native Americans of the Nipissing tribe employed as hunters.

During the ensuing years, the house, known alternately as the Chief Trader's House, the Henry House, or "Fort Kalapuya," also served as a place for trading with the local Kalapuyan Indians.

The Nipissing were among North America's finest trappers, brought west from the region of Lake Nipissing near Ontario, Canada. They were members of the Algonkin Indian family.

In addition to acting as a depot for hunting expeditions, the Willamette Post also gathered large stores of game for shipment to the always food-deprived residents of Fort George.

Established by British law, the North West Company and the Hudson's Bay Company merged in 1821 and began operating under the name of the latter.

By the late 1820s, the Willamette Post was still intact as French-Indian families began to settle around Champoeg and in a small community that would become known as St. Paul.

In the decade of the 1830s, the post and surrounding property began transitioning to new owners and new usage: farming

Pierre Bellique, a French Canadian fur trapper turned farmer, and his wife Genevieve, lived here. Etienne Lucier settled near Bellique. The two would become the first true non-native farmers in the history of the Oregon Country.

Later, Joshua George Eberhard, Ken Austin's grandfather, bought 720 acres of the historic property. This happened sometime around 1860. Austin is co-founder and co-owner of Newberg's dental manufacturing company, A-dec.

Joshua moved into what remained of the Henry House. It was a 12-by-12-foot dwelling that stood one and a half stories high and was outfitted with glass windows and clapboard walls.

When the Willamette River flooded in 1861, it washed away everything in its path, including the town of Champoeg and most of what remained of the old post. From the Henry House, Joshua managed to save the fireplace mantle.

In a new house he built on higher ground in the late 1860s, Joshua installed the mantle. Today, the Eberhard House survives intact, although it has been expanded over time to accommodate growing families. It is still in its original location: Old Champoeg Road, one-half mile east of Hwy 219.

The mantle is there, although the bottom sections on both sides are replacement boards, necessary repairs due to heat over time eating away the originals.

For many years, Joshua's broadax stayed close to the fireplace. When it was stolen, it was replaced with a look-alike. ❖

The contributions of the Metis

In this story we examine a people who flourished through the first part of the 19th century in that part of the Willamette Valley we refer to as French Prairie. This culture was primarily composed of French Canadian trappers, at one time employed by the Hudson's Bay Company at Fort Vancouver, and their Native American wives. Included were the offspring of these unions.

The French word *metis* (pronounced "matee") is often used to describe them. Before the American Civil War (1861-65), the word for mixed-race individuals was *mestee*.

Near Newberg, the Metis people generally lived in small cabins on home sites scattered throughout the present-day communities of Champoeg and St. Paul.

Elsewhere, other locations hosting these families included what we know today as Charbonneau, Gervais, St. Louis and everything to the city limits of Keizer.

By the late 1820s, the Metis had become the dominant population group in the area, surpassing many of the Native American tribes whose presence in the Willamette Valley had extended back for centuries.

Oregon historians generally believe the role of the Metis in the settlement and economic history of the Oregon Territory has never been fully appreciated. This is particularly evident in the agricultural development of the Willamette Valley, often and mistakenly attributed to the first settlers who came here from the east via the Oregon Trail.

The truth is, between 1829 and 1843, successful Metis agricultural communities were already flourishing in the heart of the French Prairie.

Put another way, when the Great Migration wagon train arrived in Oregon City in 1843, it was not greeted by a virgin wilderness but a settled landscape whose population had already discovered the agricultural strategies needed to successfully farm the valley.

This helps explain why the Jason Lee Mission bypassed the richness of French Prairie to settle close to Salem (Willamette Mission State Park, north of Keizer). All the best land to the north had been taken.

What caused the Metis to be largely forgotten is a research topic that has been a source of fascination to archeologist David Brauner at Oregon State University in Corvallis for the past 30 years.

In an interview I did with him a few years ago, Brauner gave me his explanation for what finally happened to the Metis.

"They were illiterate," he said, "so they didn't chronicle their history, dreams, aspirations and goals for the future."

"They spoke French, their own jargon, native languages, but not English. They were viewed by most Americans as being Indian. On the other hand, having worked for the Hudson's Bay Company, many Americans viewed them as British.

"Most of all, they were Catholic, a religion abhorred by the increasingly dominant Protestant population pouring into the valley."

The result of all this, he said, was that throughout the 1840s and 1850s, the French Canadian/Metis land base began to diminish.

He concluded: "In the end, social and cultural incompatibility, exclusionary land claim laws and Indian removal policies were foremost in separating them from their highly coveted land."

Today, the only perceived impact of the Metis population on Oregon history is with a few scattered place names, small communities that still dot the landscape. ❖

Our local "rock star" of the fur trade

In the later stages of his life, French Canadian Étienne Lucier (1793-1853) lived just across the Willamette River south of Newberg in the vicinity of the Willamette Post, close enough to the "Grubby End" for us to claim him as one of our own.

This is good because he remains a most fascinating and important early settler in the Oregon Country in the early 1800s.

Indeed, Lucier is so famous we'll only briefly review his accomplishments before moving to a discussion of certain other aspects of his life not generally known, but which for me hold great fascination.

Born in 1793 in the Montreal region of Lower Canada (Quebec), Monsieur Lucier, a fur trapper by profession, joined the Wilson Price Hunt Party of the (John Jacob) Astor Expedition (1810-1812) that journeyed overland to the mouth of the Columbia River to help establish Fort Astoria for Astor's Pacific Fur Company. This places him in the vanguard of the earliest Indo-European settlers to the Oregon County after the Lewis and Clark Expedition.

If this isn't fame enough, some web sources put him among the first of the trappers to reside (if only briefly) in that location which eventually became the city of Portland. This happened sometime around 1828.

On May 2, 1843, as the story goes, he was one of two French Canadians (F.X. Matthieu the other) to vote in favor of organizing a provisional government for the Oregon Country at the legendary Champoeg meeting held that day.

This action helped lay the groundwork toward U.S. territorial status granted to the region by Congress in 1848.

Lucier is also generally considered to be Oregon's first farmer.

When he died on March 8, 1853, at age 60, he was buried in St. Paul, where he remains. He was married twice and fathered five children.

Now a new book by writer Peter Stark, released March 2014 under the title, *Astoria: Astor and Jefferson's Lost Pacific Empire*, places men such as Lucier in a context I've never seen.

In short, the French Canadian fur trapper (*coureur des bois*) of the 19th century, of which Lucier was a card-carrying member, held sway over the public's attention and imagination like rock stars do in our own day.

Clearly, star power was what was going on that summer Sunday in 1810 as the first recruits for the Astor Expedition came down the Hudson River toward the clustered docks that sat at the southern tip of Manhattan Island.

Hundreds of spectators crowded the space to see this great vessel of the North, a 40-foot birch-bark canoe powered by nine French Canadian voyageurs who had paddled from Montreal.

The masterful storyteller that he is, Stark pictures the scene as if he had been there:

"They came alongside the docks (and) *could barely find a spot to land. They were short men—few over five feet six—the better to fold their legs into cargo-jammed canoes. Their upper bodies bulged with outsized strength.* (Once ashore) *two of the voyageurs reached down, one at the bow and one at the stern, and plucked* (the canoe) *out of the water and easily slung the giant, dripping hull on their shoulders. The crowd gasped with astonishment at their strength."*

Six-feet wide, the Montreal Canoe these supermen commanded, or *canot du maitre* as it was known, could haul up to four tons of fur. For two centuries, this boat was the fastest mode of transportation into the wilderness of the North American continent. Propelled at six miles an hour for up to 15 hours at a sitting, distances of 90 miles a day were routine.

During portages around falls and other rough spots in the rivers, a typical voyageur could haul a staggering 180 pounds of fur pelts on his back, using a special tumpline or harness worn on top of the head near the hairline.

As the buffalo was nature's perfect beast for the American prairie, the French Canadian fur trapper was, by custom, culture and training, the perfect human for employing the wilderness to make a living.

Although other nationalities—African-American, English, Spanish, and especially the Scots—roamed the vastness of the American West in search of pelts, nothing they did, Stark reports, quite compared to the French voyageur for sheer moxie. When financial giant John Jacob Astor insisted that Hunt give preference to hiring Americans for the rigorous trip, there were loud objections all around.

The best chance for success, they said, would be to employ the more experienced French Canadian "Northwesters."

Little wonder, then, that Hudson's Bay Company Chief Factor John McLoughlin (at Fort Vancouver) hired scores of voyageurs to work the beaver streams and rivers of the Far West; or that, after the 1830s, we would have so many of these rock stars of fur living out their retirement years on that section of the Willamette Valley known to us as the French Prairie. ❖

The world they left behind

Michael Laframbois, Robert "Doc" Newell, Joseph Pin, Ewing Young... their names around Newberg are legend.

Just across the Willamette River, dozens of retired employees of the Hudson's Bay Company lived and thrived on the land we know as French Prairie.

South of Woodburn, we find Joseph and Jean Baptiste Gervais of Geravis, Oregon fame.

Elsewhere, say hello to Joe and Stephen Meek, Moses "Black" Harris, Joseph Gale, Osborne Russell and Tom Fitzpatrick

In addition to the role all these men played in the early settlement of pioneer Oregon, there was one other thing they held in common.

Before they were Oregonians, before they hired out as guides to the pioneers traveling the Oregon Trail, they were mountain men of the Rocky Mountain fur trade.

In days long ago, beaver pelts were in huge demand all over the world, their popularity due to how they were used in the making of hats and coats for men and women of high fashion.

The American West was a rich source for beaver. Mountain men roamed the creeks, rivers and lakes of the western states setting their traps. Most worked for one of three companies: the American Fur Company, the Hudson's Bay Company or the Rocky Mountain Fur Company.

Prices were so high, a year or two of high yield could make a man wealthy. The industry climaxed during the years 1825-1840, then gradually disappeared.

When it was over, when the supply of beaver had finally been exhausted, many of these trappers came to the northern Willamette Valley to settle down, leaving behind a lifestyle that has since become a source of fascination to historians.

Although eyewitness accounts of the period are rare, we are lucky to have published several which have become popular (from the Indo-European perspective): Lewis Garrard's *Wah To Yah & The Taos Trail* and George Frederick Ruxton's *Life in the Far West*. Bernard DeVoto's *Across the Wide Missouri,* first published in 1947, is also a standard reference for the "West that was" and is based on the two books above.

What they tell is the story of the world the mountain men left behind. It's a version of the West radically different from what's come down to us from Hollywood. Here are several of my favorite examples:

Buffler: This was how the mountain men pronounced the word "buffalo." Life on the plains, for both the trappers and Native Americans, was, according to Ruxton, a buffalo culture, in which the giant beasts were used for clothing, food, fuel, shelter and everything in between. Buffalo meat for the trapper was viewed as a complete diet and trappers were not delicate eaters. The entrails (*boudins*) and liver were considered delicious, often eaten raw right after the kill. Buffalo meat was also used to make pemmican, a high energy survival food highly prized during the dead of winter. In "starving times," mountain men ate young dogs, panther, boiled beaver tails, their lariats and moccasins. Buffalo brains were rubbed on buffalo hides to soften them.

Coupling: Once the weather turned frigid cold, it was common practice for mountain men to sleep together as a way of staying warm. Arriving by horseback at the location of that night's camp, each "couple" would chose their spot before they dismounted. Today, the practice of snuggling next to someone else for body heat is often referred to as "spooning."

Forting up: Iconic in the Hollywood Western movies are the countless scenes of settlers "circling the wagons" to discourage Indian attacks. Mountain men referred to this as "forting up," which translated meant to prepare to fight a defensive battle. DeVoto recounts that in 1832, not far from Pierre's Hole (across the mountains from Jackson Hole and within sight of the Grand Tetons), a large band of Gros Ventres warriors drew into a grove of willows and built a breastwork of fallen trees, then dug foxholes behind it. There they waited for the mountain men to attack. Lewis Garrard recounts that a popular landmark on the Santa Fe Trail was Pawnee Fort, in which a war party of Pawnees had fortified themselves when besieged by a hostile tribe.

Words and expressions: Ruxton's book remains one of the best sources available for the colorful language of the fur trade. We still use a lot of their words and expressions today: to be "buffaloed" was to be confused; a "greenhand (horn)" was someone with no experience; "I'm dry" meant you were looking for something stronger than water; a "flash in the pan" was a man who spent a lot of time bragging about things he couldn't back up; if your "lights went out," you had died; potatoes were "spuds," a "possibles bag" was a leather bag used to carry personal items; a "gully washer" was a heavy downpour.

Said DeVoto about this very special breed of men:

"The mountain men were a tough race...their courage, skill and mastery of the conditions of their chosen life were absolute or they would not have been here. Nor would they have been here if they had not responded to the loveliness of the country and found in their way of life something precious beyond safety, gain and comfort...." ❖

Ewing Young

Permanent settlement of Newberg and vicinity begins with the arrival of Ewing Young in the fall of 1834. This event predates the issuance of the first Provisional Land Claims in Yamhill County by almost a decade.

Born circa 1794-1799 (the date was never documented), the six-foot-two Tennessean spent his early adult years as a fur trapper and trader on the western frontier. In the early 1820s, he worked the Missouri River region. Later, he traveled the Santa Fe Trail and helped open the Southwest to trapping. He moved north to Oregon from California after leading the first American trapping expedition to reach the Pacific Coast from New Mexico.

His death in February 1841 without an heir exposed the fact the Oregon territory had no legal means to handle the disposition of property. This event played a significant role in the formation of the Oregon Provisional Government two years later at Champoeg.

In-between his arrival and passing, he accomplished much to help establish our city and state.

The year he made his first venture into this area, he brought a large number of horses and mules to the Willamette Valley. In doing so, he became Oregon's first rancher.

To get here, he followed a route known by various names, including the Hudson's Bay Company Pack Trail, the Overland Trail, the Applegate Trail, the Old California Trail, and more recently, the Ewing Young Trail. Credit for exploring the route (using Native American and animal trails) goes to Peter Skene Ogden, Joseph Gervais, John Work and Michel LaFramboise. Peter Ogden founded Ogden, Utah. LaFramboise was among Newberg's earliest settlers. His Provisional Land Claim between Parrett Mountain and the Willamette River was filed in 1846, on a homestead he staked out in 1840.

Historians Ken Munford and Charlotte Wirfs, writing for Oregon State University's Horner Museum Tour Guide Series in 1981, give what is still the best description of the way Young and his companions entered West Chehalem.

"After fording La Creole (Rickreall) Creek at present Dallas, the pack trail (heading north) *easily crossed rolling plains and flat prairies to the Yamhill River. The rocky ledge that made falls on the Yamhill also provided firm footing for horses and cattle crossing the river. Skirting or crossing western spurs of the Red Hills of Dundee and eight miles north of the falls of the Yamhill, they found a 'veritable horse heaven.' Here on a lush prairie dotted with shady oaks he turned the trail weary horses and mules out to pasture and* (made) *his home."*

This was the first such structure built by a settler on the west banks of the Willamette. But where was it?

Evidence suggests there may have been more than one location and possibly as many as three. The first was at spot on the Willamette River across from Champoeg. The second would have been near the mouth of Chehalem Creek. Here, he built lumber and grist mills. The third, the home site where he died, was toward Yamhill-Carlton, four miles west of Newberg.

A thorough study done in 1987 by Infotech Research of Eugene places this last location near the intersection of King's Grade with North Valley Road. Nearby sits the legendary oak tree under which the famous trapper is reportedly buried.

Archeological digs at the site have yielded hundreds of pottery and glassware bits, nails, buttons, broken tobacco pipe stems, and much more, all period-correct. A strong oral tradition also links the location to Young.

In 1837, Young traveled to California by ship and returned overland with over 600 head of cattle. He used them to help break the Hudson's Bay Company's (at Fort Vancouver on the Columbia River) monopoly on beef stock. To do so, he helped form a small business conglomerate known as the Willamette Cattle Company.

Ironically, his list of partners included HBC Chief Factor John McLoughlin. Others were Methodist missionary Rev. Jason Lee, James O'Neil, Webley John Hauxhurst, William J. Bailey, and George Gay, all of whom participated in the May 1843 Champoeg meeting to create a provisional government for the region. Lee is also a founder of Willamette University.

Gay, a former English sailor, (1810-1882), reportedly built the first brick structure west of the Rocky Mountains on the future Yamhill-Polk County line south of Dayton. Gay's great-grandson was 1950s Rock and Roll idol, Johnny Ray. Ray's million-seller records included "Cry," (with The Four Lads) and "The Little White Cloud that Cried."

At his passing (from chronic stomach problems), Young was the wealthiest settler in the Oregon territory.

Ewing Young lived in Oregon less than 10 years. In that short amount of time, he left behind two of our most enduring pioneer legacies. In life, he brought together missionaries, American, English, Hudson's Bay Company and French Canadian settlers to work toward the building of a state. In death, he provided the catalyst that led directly to the nascent beginnings of our government.

Returning to Munford and Wirfs, they wrote this lasting tribute to our intrepid pioneer:

"Young and the men he attracted to Yamhill County represent the nucleus of the first settlement of Americans in the Willamette Valley. He demonstrated for those who came

later that courage, resourcefulness, energy, and enterprise were elements in building a prosperous commonwealth in a far western wilderness. He also illustrated that one cannot take acid for indigestion and expect to live to a ripe old age."

Here in the city, a park at the end of S. Blaine is named for Young, along with an elementary school west on North Valley Road. ❖

Here come the pioneers!

It's now time to turn our attention to the early 1840s, when the "Grubby End" witnesses settlers in the numbers it takes to grow a place from a scattering of homesteads into a real town.

It's also important to outline several government programs dating from 1843-1855, in which land in Washington, Idaho and Oregon was given away as a means of settling the Pacific Northwest.

Before such programs, folks simply found a location they liked and dug in. Establishing a claim came about rather primitively, for example, using a creek or distant hill to set boundaries.

An honor system prevailed: if you don't bother my claim, I won't bother yours. Sounds simple enough, right? But there was a problem: no one legally owned anything.

Enter Oregon's first provisional government, crudely formed at Champoeg in May 1843. It drafted Oregon's first constitution, the "Organic Law of the Provisional Government of Oregon."

Approved on July 5, 1843, it authorized Provisional Land Claims (PLCs) not to exceed 640 acres for married couples. Claims under the new law were granted at the federal land office in Oregon City.

In 1850, the Donation Land Claim Act (DLCA) became the new law and brought thousands of additional settlers to the Willamette Valley.

Hillsboro's Samuel R. Thurston (1815-1851), Oregon's territorial delegate to Congress, fathered the DLCA. When it was passed on Sept. 27, 1850, it granted 160 acres to every unmarried white male 18 or older; 320 acres to every married couple arriving before Dec. 1, 1850.

If claimants could show proof of working and improving the land for five consecutive years, the total was boosted to 640 acres for married couples. Wives could own their halves in their own names, a first for the United States.

The long and the short of all this is obvious: Provisional Land Claims are older than Donation Land Claims. Dating the earliest arrivals to Newberg requires use of the PLCs, not the DLCs.

It is important to remember that settlers had an "arrival" date, meaning their arrival in Oregon, an "occupancy" date for occupying a piece of ground, and a "settled claim" date, that is, when their piece was actually theirs in the eyes of the law.

Often, folks tended to "squat" for a time, a trial period if you will, before doing anything more binding (filing a claim). Also, it was possible to settle a claim before occupancy, so determining true residency can be tricky.

For example, on the southeast of what would one day be Newberg, Provisional Land Claim records kept by the Yamhill County Historical Society in Lafayette show that French Canadians Michael and Emily La Framboise (also La Frumbois), married in 1838, arrived in Newberg in 1840, but didn't receive official status on their claim until either December 1846 or January 20, 1846.

After Michael and Emily, here's a snapshot-in-time of the earliest pioneers to live in the Newberg area.

The earliest PLC occupancy date which this writer could find for our part of the county was issued to Sidney Smith on Feb. 28, 1845. This was more than five years after his arrival in West Chehalis (four miles west of Newberg) in 1839.

The date for French Canadian Gideon Gravel's PLC is Dec. 5, 1845. But when did he first locate to the area? Next in line is Joseph Pin, an old Hudson's Bay man, who dates to Dec. 18, 1845.

Another early example is found in the person of Joseph Hess, clearly one of the first (if not the first) Oregon Trail pioneers to choose the "Grubby End" as home. Hess came here with his wife Mary on Christmas Eve 1843, maybe even before Gravel or Pin. But Hess doesn't receive occupancy status on his PLC until July 11, 1846, and doesn't settle it until Nov. 20, 1847.

The Hess family traveled west with the "Great Migration" wagon train in 1843.

Stories about this colorful man abound, one of which is that Joseph and Mary squatted in a tent on the banks of the creek that bears their name for at least a year before moving into more permanent quarters. Their original claim was located northwest of downtown along Highway 240. Later, they would buy William Wallace's DLC north of Springbook.

Clearly, by the 1840s, the arrivals include a mix of French Canadians and Oregon Trail pioneers attracted to the north side of the Willamette River from places such as Champoeg and St. Paul.

Keep in mind, the names under review here are those who arrive before, not after, the Donation Land Claim Act of 1850. Or they file land claims prior to 1850. Therefore, this list would not include some of the more prominent families of early Newberg such as Brutscher, Parrish or Robertson.

As for the Canadians, their dates include Michel Placide (later known as Laferte), March 24, 1846, whose Provisional Land Claim became the nucleus of Joseph Rogers' claim and whose river landing, known in the beginning as "Placide's Landing," was an early landmark and precursor to Rogers Landing; and Baptiste DeGuire, whose dates are unknown but who clearly was living near the mouth of Chehalem Creek before 1847, on land which he would soon sell to David Ramsey, an important early icon in Newberg's history.

By 1847 or 1848, "Rogers Landing" or "Rogers Ferry" had replaced "Placide's Landing" as the name folks used to designate the location. A store and ferry were now operating to give the place a more permanent feel. When it came time for Rogers to plat a town, he chose "Chehalem." Locals also referred to the place as "Chehalem City."

In mapping out the town, Rogers was assisted by Sam Snowden, a neighbor originally from England. Pioneer Elisah McDaniel lived nearby. The plat was finished on Feb. 19, 1848, then filed at Oregon City on June 13. Historians today use both "Rogers Landing" and "Chehalem" as early names for Newberg, as was the custom back in the day. Rogers' death in 1855 put an end to his dream.

Other early settlers to Newberg include Charles and Amanda Fendall (daughter of Lewis Rogers), who arrive on Oct. 13, 1843, but who don't settle their land claim until June 12, 1852; Nathan K. Sitton, who arrives with the Fendalls but who eventually settles on the north fork of the Yamhill River with his Dec. 1, 1848, PLC; John and Susan Williamson, who also settle the area in 1843 but who don't see their claim approved until May 15, 1852; David Layfield, who dates to 1845, then sells his land claim to Daniel Deskins in January 1848; Green C. Rogers, who enters the area in 1845 and receives a DLC in 1852; Daniel Dodge Bayley and his wife, Elizabeth, who land in West Chehalem in 1845 and take their claim on March 7, 1848; and Clark Rogers, who arrives in 1846 and receives official status in March 1847.

Additional early names include Lewis Rogers, October 1846; George Stephen Nelson and wife Margaret Nelson, who date to 1844 and settle their claim on March 15, 1845; Levi Hagie (Hagey), with a PLC occupancy of July 7, 1847, and a settled claim date in December 1850; the already mentioned Joe Rogers; John and Susan Williamson, Sept. 23, 1847; Charles Patton, the same year; Amelia Welch, who settles her claim on March 30, 1846, and her son, John Welch, who settles his on Dec. 20, 1846; James Rogers, March 20, 1847; Richard and Jane Everest, who apply for their claim in November 1847; Daniel Dodge Bayley and Elizabeth Munson Bayley, who arrive in 1845 but who don't secure their land claim until March 7, 1848; and finally Timothy Bayley, their son, who takes up his PLC the same year.

According to tradition, David Ramsey and Susan Shuck Ramsey, daughter of Jacob Shuck, build the first frame house in the Newberg area on a knoll west of Chehalem Creek and south of present-day Dayton Avenue. In 1849, Ramsey and Joe Rogers begin operating a sawmill along Chehalem Creek near the Ramsey house. In 1877 the operation converts to a grist mill.

In 1929, before a meeting of the Newberg Chamber of Commerce, local historian Perry D. Macy, a professor at then Pacific College (now George Fox University), said there were only a handful of families living in the area by 1845 and that most of these early settlers went into the cattle business because of the abundance of grasslands and lack of trees in this part of Yamhill County.

This went on, he reported, until the time of the California Gold Rush in 1849 and was Newberg's earliest industry. "The gold rush changed everything," he added. "Most of the men got the fever and went to look for gold. Those who stayed behind, however, made more (in most cases) than those who went.

"An example is that one man sold four boxes of apples for $500. Eggs were sold to a ship captain for 60 cents a dozen. He took them to San Francisco and resold them for a dollar apiece.

"In the restaurants eggs were $2 each. The story was told of one man who paid such a price for an egg and then couldn't eat it. Farmers began raising wheat and other farm crops." ❖

Sidney Smith's schoolmarm daughter

L et's have some fun with an early pioneer settler and his schoolmarm daughter. His name was Sidney Smith. He was born in Amsterdam, New York, October 1809.

In 1839, Smith signed up as a member of the ill-fated Peoria Party and was the first in the group to reach Oregon. This was probably in early September of that same year.

He next came to the Willamette Valley, where he put down stakes in Marion County before moving to Yamhill County. Arrivals of settlers to the vicinity of the "Grubby End" pre-1843 are rare so this is important.

Smith eventually became an employee of Ewing Young and settled near Young's cabin four miles west of Newberg.

The Peoria Party would make a great movie. Numbering 19 men, the group formed themselves into a quasi-military unit known as the Oregon Dragoons. They headed west out of Peoria, Ill., in May 1839, to help colonize the Oregon Country on behalf of the United States.

Their real mission was to attract enough American settlers to the territory to drive out the English fur trading companies still operating in the Pacific Northwest. They carried with them a flag which read, "Oregon or the Grave."

The more they traveled, the more the word "grave" seemed like their fate. The weather was terrible, food was short, and so were their tempers. Smith, for example, pulled a gun during a heated exchange and accidentally shot himself. The party began to disintegrate. Some returned to Illinois. Only nine made it to Oregon.

Sidney Smith would eventually become a wealthy rancher, after having made $3,000 in the gold fields of California in the late 1840s. He voted in favor of a Provisional Government for the Oregon Territory at Champoeg in May 1843. He died at his home in Lafayette, Sept. 18, 1880.

However, he lived long enough to watch his daughter, Irene, become a schoolmarm at the collegiate level, first at Philomath College in 1872, then at Corvallis College (now Oregon State University) a year later. Here, she had the responsibility of supervising the school's preparatory department for its younger students. She would hold the position until June 1875.

Among the new rules drafted by Ms. Smith (who was actually married to a local doctor named Calbreath) was this curious dictate: "All communications between ladies and gentlemen on the college premises are expressly forbidden."

According to Benton County historian John E. Smith, in his priceless little pamphlet, *Corvallis College,* published in 1953, "…Miss Smith was trained in a very strict girls' school (St. Mary's Academy in Portland). Although the rule remained in the college catalog for more than a decade, there seems to be little or no evidence that its enforcement was ever attempted after she left the college." ❖

"Boys, don't leave me!"

There's a small family graveyard between here and Carlton that in 1856 was the scene of the largest military funeral in Yamhill County history.

On April 20 of that year, nearly 1,000 Oregonians trekked to this lovely spot to pay their respects to a man who had lost his life fighting the Yakima Indians near Toppenish, Wash.

When you consider that less than 2,000 people lived in Yamhill County during the mid-1850s, that's 50 percent of the county's entire population. If this funeral were held today, and the percentages were to stay the same, it would take a venue the size of Autzen Stadium to handle the crowd.

The small plot, surrounded by an ancient fence, sits off the Bayliss Road on a farm once belonging to the deceased, but now in the respectful hands of a family whose descendants have been here since 1844. It is not open to the public.

As part of the family's oral tradition, passed from generation to generation for almost a century and a half, it is said that when the casket arrived at the gravesite, wagons, buggies and horses carrying the respectful were still leaving communities five miles away.

The soldier in question was Absalom Jefferson Hembree. Known affectionately as "Uncle Abb," he was born in December 1813 in middle Tennessee and crossed the plains to Oregon in 1843. Hembree, his wife Nancy (nee Dodson), their four children and other traveling companions, were in the vanguard of a westward expansion of followers of the Restoration Movement, a splinter group of Baptists (also Disciples of Christ) dedicated to ridding Christianity of denominational creeds and working toward unifying all believers into one church.

In this same group was friend William T. Newby, the man who platted a town not far from the Hembree farm and named it after his (Newby's) hometown, also back in Tennessee…McMinnville!

Hembree, who raised livestock and owned a store in Lafayette, became a leader among the Baptist faithful in the county. He also served five terms in the Oregon Provisional and Territorial legislatures as the representative from Yamhill County.

In 1851 he became director of the ill-fated Portland and Valley Plank Road Company. When bankruptcy forced its closure, he helped organized the Pacific Telegraph Company to improve communication between Oregon and California.

However, it is his military career that most interests us for this story.

Hembree was the commanding officer of Co. E of the 1st Oregon Mounted Volunteers, one of eight such companies assembled in late 1855 in answer to Governor George L. Curry's call for men to help fight in the Yakima War (1855-1858) in Washington State.

The unit was headquartered at Fort Dalles near an original campsite of the Lewis & Clark Expedition in the small settlement of The Dalles.

In our state's history, only three military organizations are older: the First Oregon Riflemen (1847-1848); Independent Rifle Ranges (1850); and the Regional Volunteer Units, which served from 1852-1854.

Co. E was not only assembled by Hembree, it was the first such company mustered in to service. This happened in Portland on Oct. 11, 1855. Initially, there were 102 men under his command, including two of his nephews.

The company spent the winter months in the Walla Walla Valley. Conditions were miserable. As winters go, this was a bad one, with ice on the Columbia preventing supplies from getting through and forcing the men to eat their horses to survive. Finding replacement mounts became a top priority.

On the morning of April 10, Captain Hembree was leading a scouting party near the confluence of Satus Creek and the Yakima River when they spotted what appeared to be a group of riderless horses headed in their direction.

The scene quickly turned to ambush. Indian warriors hidden on the opposite sides of the horses began firing. Hembree was hit and fell to the ground. As his men fled they could hear him yelling, "Boys, don't leave me."

Alone now, Yamhill's finest didn't stand a chance. He was scalped, mutilated and stripped naked. Later, his men returned to retrieve the body.

Rather than bury him where he had died, his remains were placed on a litter stretched between two mules and carried back to the Columbia River. Due to high winds, the party had to wait two days to cross.

In The Dalles, he was put in a large box and packed in ice. The steamer *Columbia Belle* took him to Portland. At the Yamhill River, the trip to Lafayette was by canoe. For the funeral, a handkerchief was used to conceal his loss of hair.

Today, his grave marker sits next to Nancy's and is the tallest in the cemetery. His stone faces west, looking out to one of the most spectacular views of the Coastal Range to be found anywhere. ❖

QUAKERS

Arrival of the Quakers to Oregon

Newberg's important connection to the Society of Friends (Quakers) begins in the 1870s. It is important for our understanding of Newberg's past to discuss this relationship in some detail.
Here's why.

With apologies to Joseph Rogers, who attempted to plat a town but died (in 1855) before he could see it happen, it was the Friends who managed to bring together a loose collection of farms and other small property owners and fashion them into a real town, incorporated as such in 1889, then as a city in 1891.

Before we proceed, let's define a few terms for those not familiar with the basic organization of the Friends. A "Monthly Meeting" is the local church organization; a "Quarterly Meeting" is made up of several churches, generally five or more; the "Yearly Meeting" is made up of the monthly and quarterly meetings. These gatherings are akin to church conferences held by other Christian denominations.

Newberg is the home of the Northwest Yearly Meeting, which annually hosts representatives from 65 Society churches in Oregon, Washington and Idaho. Add to this George Fox University, one of only three Quaker-affiliated universities in the United States, and the Barclay Press, in Newberg since 1959 and the principal publications ministry for the Society, and Newberg becomes one of the most important Quaker communities in America.

According to H.S. Nedry, in an article he published in the *Oregon Historical Quarterly* titled, "The Friends Come to Oregon," the arrival in 1843 of the William Mills family from Arkansas indicates there were Quakers in Oregon during the earliest days of pioneer travel to the state.

Two years later, in 1845, the Edwin Comfort family practiced their Quaker faith in Portland. In 1848, they were joined by the Hiram Bond family. In 1850, George and Mary Stroud began Oregon's first Friends Sunday School meetings in Ashland.

Elsewhere, Robert and Sarah Lindsey were sent from the London Yearly Meeting in 1859 to California and Oregon to minister to early Quaker settlers in the Far West. They led the first Quaker meetings in California and later became the first Quaker ministers to visit Oregon.

In Salem, the charismatic couple conducted the first Friends worship meeting held in the region. They also presided over meetings in Eugene. After eight months, the Lindseys returned to London.

The name Rebecca Mendenhall Lewis also survives as an early Pacific Northwest Quaker.

In 1864 she moved to Portland to be with her daughter, Mrs. P.J. Mann, at 441 Third Street. The address is historic because it became the headquarters for all the visiting ministers who became the founders of Quakerism in Oregon. The names include Abel Bond (arrives 1866), Mary B. Pinkham (1870), Rebecca Clawson (1874), and William Hobson (1871, 1875).

Bond was from the Cottonwood Monthly Meeting in Kansas and traveled the state by foot, ministering along the way and distributing written materials.

Pinkham was from Ohio. During her first visit to Oregon, she spent several weeks holding meetings and visiting with families. She returned in 1873 to conduct a two-year ministry among the settlers.

Minister Rebecca Clawson was the leader of a party of Friends who came to Oregon in October 1874. The group included her daughter, Elizabeth White, plus her daughter's husband, Nathan. Both were to play an important role in the early history of the Friends in Yamhill County.

Remaining in Salem until 1875, the three moved to Dayton. Soon the Fuson family and son-in-law, Mason Hadley (from Indiana), moved next door and services were held in the White's home with Mrs. Clawson leading.

According to Shirley O'Neil's groundbreaking research published as *Yamhill County Pioneers: Study of the Inhabitants Listed in the 1850 Census for Yamhill County*, among the first Quakers to arrive in what would later be Newberg and vicinity were Jacob Shuck and his family, his son-in-law David Ramsey and Levi Hagey, all of whom were here by the late 1840s and who established Provisional Land Claims just east of Dundee.

Two locations are important: (1) between Newberg and Dundee on both sides of Hwy 99W (in the location known informally today as "Dunberg"); (2) along both sides of Dayton Avenue in southwest Newberg clear to the Dundee city limits. In both places, Shuck, Ramsey, Hagey and others helped established what became known as the "Quaker Community," a location responsible for all subsequent development of the Quaker influence in the "Grubby End." ❖

Newberg becomes a Quaker settlement

We now turn our attention to Newberg and fast forward to the 1870s. It is here we see enough Quaker settlers to establish a permanent home for Quakerism in the Pacific Northwest. William Hobson takes the lead in this regard and is the focus of this discussion.

Feeling the call to establish his own Monthly Meeting in California, Oregon or Washington, Hobson came west in 1870. He brought with him a keen eye for the right conditions to foster a community of believers.

Arriving first in California, he took an overland stage to Eugene, held meetings and continued to Salem, Portland and Walla Walla, Wash. Not completely satisfied with any of his visits, he returned home to Iowa beginning on June 7, 1871. He traveled by steamer from Portland for San Francisco and from there by train back to the Midwest. However, his interest in the Pacific Northwest stayed high priority.

In 1875 he was back, accompanied by (according to his diary) J.S. Bond, Perry Hadley and David J. Wood. The three stayed with the Nathan and Elizabeth White family in Dayton, where Hobson began to emerge as a forceful leader of the group.

He also continued searching for a place of his own, often traveling by foot. He went south into the heart of the Willamette Valley and over into eastern Washington. He favored the Washington location, but an early frost and the damage it had done to the peach crop changed his thinking. Back in Dayton, he now began focusing on what would later be known as the "Grubby End."

Born in Guilford County, N.C, Feb. 4, 1820, he was 55 at the time. He wasn't young, but young enough in spirit to conduct the religious work he felt was his destiny.

On Oct. 10, 1875, in Dayton, Hobson began the first *regular* gathering of Friends in the Pacific Northwest. The group continued here until March 19, 1876, then moved to the William Clemmens home in Newberg. This was the beginning of the present Newberg Monthly Meeting.

Visiting a cousin, Ester Markham, who was living on the Oliver J. Walker Donation Land Claim and whose husband had been thrown into the state pen in Salem, Hobson became intrigued enough by her 320-acre farm to buy it. It was late November 1875. The location today would be three-fourths of a mile north of E. First Street. He was now ready to go back to Iowa and move his family to their new farm.

This was done in October 1876. On the return trip Hobson was accompanied by four other families, plus his son-in-law, Henry J. Austin, Ken Austin's (co-founder of A-dec) grandfather, who was married to William's daughter, Mary.

Hobson also encouraged other Quakers living in Iowa and Indiana to move to Newberg. By 1877, many new Friends had begun to arrive and settle the area, with at least 70 Friends attending meetings, now held on the second floor of a large home David Wood had built.

The first meeting at this new location was on Oct. 11, 1877, and meetings continued here for about a year. The next organizational step took place on June 1, 1878, when the group officially became the Chehalem Monthly Meeting of Friends, under the direction of the Honey Creek Friends Meeting in Iowa. This was Oregon's first officially sanctioned Monthly Meeting of Friends. In the fall of 1878, meetings were moved to a building east of Newberg owned by John T. Smith. In size it was a modest 15-by-20 feet and so low no man could stand upright in it.

Also, the group at this time was without a pastor. Visiting ministers included Hobson; future temperance worker and Elizabeth White's mother, Rebecca Clawson; a man named John Scott, who was visiting from the Deer Creek Monthly Meeting in Maryland; and Robert W. Douglas, a missionary from Australia.

The Chehalem Monthly Meeting now had over 100 members. A new building was needed. On Aug. 3, 1878, a committee was appointed to study the possibilities. However, few of the locals had enough extra money to give to the project, so two visiting ministers from the East (Elwood Siler and Josiah Morris) offered to solicit their friends back home in Indiana for the necessary money. By the fall of 1889 enough donations were collected to erect a building, 32-by-48 feet, located on the same ground as occupied today by the Friends Cemetery on Everest Road.

In 1892, this small building was replaced by a magnificent new church known today as Newberg Friends Church. At the time it was built, its size was designed to make a statement. It still does and occupies almost a full city block at the corner of Church and Fourth streets near downtown.

This is the same ground where once stood the precursor to George Fox University, Friends Pacific Academy, which operated here from 1885 to 1891 and which had in its student body a future president of the United States, Herbert Hoover.

By 1893, there were seven monthly meetings in Washington and Oregon, with over 1,300 members. At this time the region was still under the direction of the Iowa Yearly Meeting.

On Aug. 8, 1891, Northwest Friends asked Iowa for permission to take charge of and hold its own Yearly Meeting at Newberg. Granted in September 1891 to take effect the month of June 1893, Newberg has remained the home of the Northwest Yearly Meeting for the past 118 years. William Hobson, who passed away on June 25, 1891, would have been very proud.

Completing the transition of Newberg into a real "town" required one more push, which came with the arrival in 1880 of Quaker Jesse Edwards (1849-1925), his wife, Mary Kemp Edwards (1848-1923), and their four children, Clarence J., Walter F., O.K. and Mabel. ❖

The "Father of Newberg"

As we saw in the last story, fashioning Newberg into a real "town" required one more push. This came with the arrival of Jesse Edwards (1849-1925) in September 1880, his wife, Mary Kemp Edwards (1848-1923), and their four children, Clarence J., Walter F., O.K., and Mabel.

For Jesse, home before Newberg was Hendricks County, Ind. He was born there; his lineage was by way of North Carolina, Maryland and Wales.

He and his family had journeyed to Oregon by way of Indiana, then to San Francisco. Travel for this leg of the trip was by train. Along the rails, they had to furnish their own food, which included dried meats, bread and raw vegetables carried in old flour sacks.

Boarding the steamship California, they traveled the 700 miles to Oregon through seas so rough everyone got sick. From Portland, the riverboat Orient brought them to Dayton, the only established river port town in the area.

With them were E.H. Woodward, his wife, Amanda Woodward, and their son Walter. The Woodwards would eventually buy the *Newberg Graphic* and own it from 1891-1926, with father and son serving as editor and publisher.

A passionate supporter and fund-raiser for Pacific College (now George Fox University), Amanda Woodward is one-half the name given to the university's most famous building, Wood-Mar Hall.

The two families spent the winter months of 1880-81 in Dayton, sharing the same house. As members of the Society of Friends, they had been attracted here by William Hobson's work to establish a colony of Quakers in Oregon. Jesse and William had known one another back in Indiana.

Edwards was 31 at the time. He would live in Newberg for another 45 years and establish a reputation for success that would earn him the title, "The Father of Newberg." He amassed a small fortune and his resume of achievements included mayor, banker, landowner, farmer, storekeeper, sawmill owner, grain warehouse operator, postmaster, brickmaker, co-founder of a college and early pioneer (with Clarence) in rural electricity. His plat for a town, the third in Newberg's history, was the one that stuck.

As we have already seen, the area's first attempt to start a town was by Joseph Rogers in 1848. The name he chose was "Chehalem."

The second try at platting a town, and the first to be called "Newberg," was by two enterprising young Quaker couples, William P. Ruddick, his wife Sarah, and David J. and Maggie Wood.

The four were partners in the purchase of five acres of land from Elijah Hutchens. The property had been part of the J.H. Hess Provisional Land Claim of 1846.

It was bounded by Illinois Street (now West Illinois) on the north, the railroad tracks on the south, Morton Street to the west, and Main (now North Main) to the east.

On Feb. 24, 1881, county surveyor H.S. Maloney used this acreage to plat what he called "Newberg," adopting the name Sebastian Brutscher had given his post office in 1869.

The document itself is labeled "The Original Newberg."

(*Note:* Brutscher lived east of downtown, approximately where Providence Newberg hospital is today. In naming Newberg, he was inspired by his hometown in Bavaria—Newburgh. His post office was in his home and he was the city's first postmaster.)

The Ruddick/Wood plat, as envisioned by Maloney, was filed with the county on Feb. 26, 1881.

Two weeks after their arrival, Jesse and Mary decided to ride over to the "Grubby End" in a rented horse and buggy. Quakers were settling the location and they thought they might want to be a part of it. The kids went along. In a story in the *Graphic* in 1939, Clarence gives a priceless recollection of what he saw that day in 1880.

He recalled using the old Dayton county road to Newberg (Dayton Avenue survives as a remnant but only follows the old route as far as Dundee) and said the journey was mostly through scrubby timber and stump patches, on a road that had never been graded or surfaced with hard material.

As they approached the top of a small hill just south of Chehalem Creek, everyone noticed a "substantial" pioneer residence belonging to early Newberg settler David Ramsey. An orchard and large barn stood nearby. Below the road was a "flouring" mill owned by Ramsey and powered by creek water collected behind a small dam built close to a bridge.

Crossing Chehalem Creek in a northeasterly direction, the first cultivated land they saw was near where E. First Street (historically known as the Portland Road) and School Street now intersect.

Here, a woman he remembered as "Mrs. Deskin" owned acreage to the north of Portland Road, of which she had about 12 acres planted in wheat, another 30-40 acres in other crops, the rest in second growth oak and fir. The Deskin house, he recalled, was just to the north of where Meridian Street leaves First.

Along a creek he referred to as Blair Creek (now Hess Creek), a narrow dirt road ran south down the west bank to the Willamette River, closely approximating the route followed today by Wynooski Street. Clarence said there was only one house on this road until approaching the vicinity of Rogers Landing and the old Joseph Rogers homestead, which would later become the site of the old C.K. Spaulding mill, today the SP Newsprint Co., (headquartered in the state of Georgia).

He added that with the exception of two small open fields, everything from the Deskin house to the river was scrub oak and second-growth fir.

Deskin's neighbor to the south, Peter Hagey, owned 125 acres from the original Joseph Rogers Donation Land Claim. He was using 80 of it to raise wheat.

Jesse Edwards and his family relocated here in March 1881 and shortly after bought the Hagey farm. A small house was on the property, surrounded by an orchard.

In 1881 Edwards replaced the Hagey house with a new house, known today as the Hoover-Minthorn House, 115 S. River Street, because later occupants would include a future president of the United States, Herbert Hoover, and his uncle and aunt, Henry J. and Laura Minthorn. The two had adopted Hoover as a young boy after he had lost both of his parents. It is currently the oldest house in Newberg and a national treasure. Hoover lived here from 1885-1889.

In 1883, Edwards constructed and moved to a much bigger place we know as the Jesse Edwards House, 402 S. College. In 1980 it was listed on the National Register of Historic Places. Since 1998 it has been the property of George Fox University and used as the official residence of university presidents.

In total, the "Grubby End" at this time contained less than 200 residents.

Besides platting the location which now sits at the heart of the downtown business district (more on this in a minute), his long and productive career enjoys accomplishments that did more than any other early settler to ensure the town's future. In addition to establishing a store and warehouse, he owned a sawmill, a brick company, a drain tile company and Newberg's first bank.

A word about the bricks: It was Edwards who helped establish Newberg as the "Brickmaking Capital of the Pacific Northwest" from 1895-1920.

He also played a strong role in giving birth to (with son Clarence) Newberg's first electric company. He served his church as spiritual leader and helped build the magnificent Friends Church at 307 South College, which stands at the center of Quakerism in the Pacific Northwest. He was a farmer, an educator, the mayor, served as post master and built the railroad spur on Blaine.

In 1883 Edwards put in motion his own plan for a town. Realizing his neighbors often had to travel considerable distances to get supplies, he and wife Mary hired J.C. Cooper to survey and plat a town site, the first of three they would devise to encompass everything south of First Street all the way to the river. This first plat would eventually become the heart of today's business district. It was officially registered with the county on Sept. 15, 1883.

Today, this section, which borders from First Street in the north to Fourth Street in the south, and Blain Street on the west to Wynooski on the east, is known as Edwards' "Original Town." The witnesses whose names appear on the plat are J.S. Smith, Marcus Blair, Henry Austin, and Henry's wife, Mary.

Enter William Hobson. The year was 1883 or 1884. After establishing downtown Newberg's first store with a partner named Siegler on the northeast corner of First and Main (now North Main), Hobson entered into a partnership with Edwards after Siegler had sold his half to Edwards. The new partnership became Hobson & Edwards.

Again, based on what Clarence told the *Newberg Graphic* in 1939, this was not his dad's first partnership with Hobson. Around 1882, the two had bought a warehouse south of Wynooski Street for storing grain.

"It was on the low divide along the bank of the river," Edwards remembered. "I heard my father state they took in over 125,000 bushels of wheat in one year, where it was put in sacks for shipment to Portland."

With the 1887 arrival of the Southern Pacific trains, along track routes still in use today, the neighborhood along Main Street saw a surge of growth, including several hotels, a train depot, drug and furniture stores, a tobacco shop and other small businesses.

For a time this growth along Main matched what was going on over in Edwards' "Newberg." In the latter, an embryo of a business district had begun to emerge by 1888, best described as a small clustering of wooden structures mostly located around First and School streets.

Both Edwards and Hobson suspected that if a real town was going to develop, it was going to be in proximity to where the county road from Dayton to Portland intersected with First Street, in other words right where Edwards had platted his "Newberg."

Consequently, in 1884/1885, the two partners contracted with Dr. Elias Jessup to move their Main Street building slightly eastward, to a spot just east of Center Street facing First Street. The work was done during the muddy months of winter. Very near this same location, on the east side of Center between First and Second streets, Edwards and others opened The Bank of Newberg in 1886, the town's first.

Now there were two "Newbergs," Main Street on the west side and First Street to the east, only a few blocks apart. During the decade of the 1890s, the two would be rivals, with Main Street holding an early lead.

By the turn of the century, First Street surpassed its opponent to enjoy a position it would never relinquish. The two developments simply merged at some point to form one town. ❖

The tinkerer

Resting peacefully today in a small shaded cemetery in Newberg is one of the city's most famous, although his name often draws blank stares from the uninitiated. His was Miles Lowell Edwards, the son of Clarence Edwards, the grandson of Jesse Edwards, the "Father of Newberg."

For those who *do* know something of his life and remarkable career, the one part they remember is that, along with Portland cardiologist Albert Starr, Edwards collaborated to develop the world's first efficient artificial heart valve. It has been used worldwide to save countless lives. Enjoying a reputation as a quiet tinkerer, Edwards' revolutionary heart device was developed after he had retired and when he was 60 years old. It was spawned from numerous other inventions he had to his credit in such diverse fields as lumbering, aviation and the automotive industry. When he died on April 8, 1982, in Portland at age 84, he had 63 patents registered to his name.

It's almost a miracle he lived as long as he did. He had rheumatic fever when he was 13 and then suffered with a severe recurrence when he was in his later teens. This experience taught him the potential of disease to damage the valves of the human heart and sparked a lifelong interest in using his genius to fix problems of this life-giving organ.

His rise to national fame began in 1941 while he was working as a Weyerhaeuser Timber Company engineer at its pulp plant in Longview, Wash. A few weeks after the attack on Pearl Harbor, Edwards heard that aircraft manufacturers were having difficulty pumping gasoline into airplane engines at high altitude.

For over four years, he had been working on a self-priming pump in his basement workshop. He thought maybe his new device might be modified to solve the problem of how to improve high altitude fuel flow. So he went back to tinkering to see if he could come up with a solution. To do so would require retooling his invention to produce a pump that would prevent vapor lock in aircraft fuel systems. The difference in atmospheric pressure after takeoff caused gasoline to boil and vaporize, conditions under which airplane engines failed.

In the spring of 1942, with a leave of absence from his employer, Edwards was off to the Boeing Airplane Company for further experimentation. Engineers at the company were intrigued by his work and wrote a very encouraging report. In Los Angeles, Western Gear Works heard about Edwards and invited him down for additional testing.

After a year, Thompson Products Company of Cleveland, Ohio, at that time the world's largest manufacturer of pumps for aircraft, joined the team and decided conclusively that Edwards had solved the problem. Thompson executives immediately did two things: they bought the rights to the pump and retained

Edwards as a consulting engineer. By the time of the Korean War, 85 percent of all aircraft flying around the world were equipped with pumps designed by Edwards.

Throughout most of his life and wherever he lived, Edwards liked working at home. It was from these small workshops that many of his best inventions first took shape, including one that would hold a car on a hill when the foot is off the brake, a gasoline mileage meter for cars, a turn indicator for automobiles, devices to handle flax, and the necessary instrumentation airplanes need to land in fog. He also invented a whirling wheel that effectively debarks logs.

His first heart valve was developed in 1949, but it was not until 1958 that he teamed up with Starr to put the finishing touches on the invention that has brought him his most fame, the Starr-Edwards heart valve.

Two years later, the first successful human implantation of the device was made in the person of 52-year-old Philip Amundson, who in childhood had suffered from rheumatic fever and who lived a happy and healthy life for 10 years after his historic surgery until dying from an unrelated incident.

Over the years, both Starr and Edwards have been widely honored by medical groups around the world for this life-saving contribution to medical science. Edwards is also credited with the invention of the "oxygenator," a device that acts as "lungs" during cardiovascular surgery.

The story of Starr's first meeting with Edwards is legendary.

"He was an old man when I met him," the famous doctor told Oregonian *writer Ann Sullivan in 1982. "Here he was, this guy with shaky hands, wearing sneakers and a golf jacket. I was strictly an Eastern establishment type. I remember thinking, 'I wonder if this guy's a nut?' When he left, I watched him out the window. That was my first glimmer of hope. He was driving a Cadillac. If it had been a pickup truck, that would have been the end."*

Miles Lowell Edwards was born on Jan. 18, 1898, in Newberg, a member of one of Yamhill County's most distinguished pioneer families. As we have already seen, his grandfather, Jesse Edwards, founded a permanent location for Newberg after arriving in 1880 and went on to become one of the wealthiest businessmen in the Willamette Valley.

Miles' father, Clarence, was also an inventor, building a steam engine that gave Newberg its first electricity. Throughout his life, Miles credited his father with instilling in him his inventive ways.

Miles actually began his college education at George Fox in 1919, transferring after one year to Oregon Agricultural College (now Oregon State University), where he was known around campus as having the best car on campus. "Cars were scarce in those days," a 1944 article in *The Oregon Stater* reported, "but Edwards had worked up the prize of the day."

Like his grandfather and father before him, Miles became wealthy during his lifetime. In the 1960s he founded American Edwards Laboratories in Orange County, Calif., which generated $300-$350 million in yearly, worldwide sales for local medical-related industries. Today the company is known as Edwards Lifesciences.

The company's website in the mid-2000s had this to say about its namesake and his amazing legacy:

"Less than a year after introducing the world's first commercially available replacement mitral valve, Edwards and Starr debuted its aortic counterpart. These innovations spawned a company, Edwards Laboratories, which went on to launch a number of additional "firsts" in medical technology. Continuing Edwards' practice of collaborating with leading clinicians in the medical field, Edwards Laboratories worked with cardiologists Jeremy Swan and William Ganz to develop the first hemodynamic monitoring system for critically ill patients, and with vascular surgeon Thomas Fogarty to launch the first catheter technology to remove blood clots from the limbs. The Swan-Ganz and Fogarty brands of product lines became highly successful and still maintain worldwide leadership positions in their respective areas today.

"In 1966, Edwards Laboratories was purchased by American Hospital Supply Corporation and continued its pioneering work by developing and introducing its Carpentier-Edwards brand product line of replacement heart valves and heart valve repair products. Today, the Carpentier-Edwards heart valves, made of porcine and pericardial tissue, are the most widely prescribed tissue replacement valves in the world.

"In 1985, Baxter International Inc. purchased American Hospital Supply and established the Edwards organization as its CardioVascular Group. The CardioVascular Group, eager to transform itself into an even more successful business, became an independent cardiovascular company in 2000. Management and employees considered thousands of options for the name of the new company and at the end of the day, there was one clear choice. The legacy of quality and innovation established years before by Lowell Edwards made Edwards Lifesciences the overwhelming favorite.

"Edwards Lifesciences was 'reborn' when it was spun off from Baxter and its stock began trading on the New York Stock Exchange in 2000. Every employee became an owner in the company, sharing in the pride and entrepreneurial spirit that Lowell Edwards must have felt when he started his revolutionary heart valve project more than 40 years earlier."

Miles Edwards began his career with Bingham Pump Company in Portland in 1925, where he rose to the position of vice president. From 1937 to 1948 he served as plant engineer for Weyerhaeuser. In 1964, he received the American Medical Association's Distinguished Service Award for Laymen. That same year, he shared

OSU's Distinguished Service Award with Linus Pauling (OAC, Class of 1922), and Ernest Wiegand, who helped develop the maraschino cherry.

He was very devoted to George Fox University throughout his life and served on the school's Board of Trustees for over 17 years. In 1963, he was named GFU's "Alumnus of the Year." In 1969, he and his wife, Margaret (Watt), a native of Portland and a 1927 OAC graduate, established a scholarship fund at George Fox that annually provides scholarships to students interested in science or health-related professions. In 1976, he gave an additional $100,000 to GFU, at that time one of the largest private donations ever made to the university.

Margaret died in 2000 and was considered locally as an outstanding historian of the old Oregon country. She authored five books on local history, including one about her husband titled, *Miles Lowell Edwards*.

They are buried side-by-side in Newberg's Friends Cemetery near many other members of the Edwards family tree. His small gravestone sits flat to the ground with but one small inscription to describe his remarkable life: "Co-inventor of heart valves." ❖

Two women who helped save a college

In the years I've been researching local history, I've never encountered two more remarkable community visionaries than Amanda Woodward and Evangeline Martin.

Some of us have some knowledge of their historic connections to George Fox University, but how many know the details of their help in funding construction of the gorgeous Wood-Mar Hall in 1910-11?

And what did the new campus building, named for them with an ingenious combining of their last names, mean at the time to the struggling Quaker College?

In 1911, when 35-year-old Levi Pennington was chosen to replace Acting President William Reagan, the outgoing administrator warned the new president the job would not be easy.

"It has been unusually hard to make ends meet," he told Pennington, "and we are about three months behind on salaries (actually, the faculty had not been paid for three months). You will be head janitor and the head janitor gets to do all the extras."

The school was clearly in survival mode. And it wasn't just paychecks providing the pressure.

The National Education Association, in cooperation with the U.S. Bureau of Educational Standards, had established minimum requirements for colleges wanting to be recognized as "legitimate institutions of higher learning." Today we call this "accreditation."

One of the requirements was an endowment valued at $100,000 or better.

For Pennington, such an endowment would require not only the financial resources of Quakers from around the Pacific Northwest, but also across the country, especially back east, where significant monies within Quaker families were held.

The task of raising the money had started under Reagan and his belief that it probably wasn't going to happen without a new building, something so impressive it would convince donors the college had a future and was worthy of serious investment.

Newberg Graphic Editor and Publisher Ezra H. Woodward, Amanda's husband, agreed and used the power of his newspaper to push the argument: "The building makes possible an appeal to friends…as a pledge of our faith in our own institution. Those behind this movement…feel that no step has been taken that gives more assurance of an endowment…. A new brick building…will be evidence of permanence and will inspire confidence."

Estimates were put forth the building would cost $30,000 ($600,000 today).

A mass meeting was held in February 1910 to raise the amount from the local citizenry. They pledged $19,000, leaving a balance of $11,000.

Enter Evangeline and Amanda to put the finishing touches to the campaign.

Riding a buggy pulled by a horse affectionately known as "Faithful Old Kit," the two went door to door soliciting donations. By July, it was done, with money to spare.

Could it have happened without them?

Probably not.

It took Herculean energy to do what they did. They also had "style." Their use of the horse and buggy was sheer genius.

Consider this. The automobile had arrived in Newberg eight years earlier. The first was a White Steamer local resident Semon Madson had brought to town sometime around 1902. At the 1910 Fourth of July parade, representatives of the Pacific College faculty rode in an auto owned and driven by H.C. Dixon, a local physician. The well-heeled had them. Presumably the Woodwards were in this group.

My point? If you're asking for money, look like you need it. Canvassing the community in a "mechanical horse" would have seemed too ostentatious to have had much fundraising credibility.

The two women also enjoyed perfect timing. By 1910, Newberg was bursting with pride. The city's first real high school building on Sixth Street was in the works, a new home for First National Bank was being constructed at the corner of First and Washington streets, agriculture was booming, and Newberg was rightly proud of its image as the "brickmaking capital" of Oregon. It wasn't about to let its local college go under.

Taking advantage of this growing community spirit, Amanda Woodward and Evangeline Martin used it to pull off the first great coming together of the "Grubby End" in its history.

Even as Wood-Mar Hall was under construction, President Pennington announced a campaign to build a permanent endowment for the college. The goal was set at $100,000, which was reached on New Year's Eve, 1914. ❖

Levi Pennington

For over 120 years, George Fox University has been blessed with gifted presidents, beginning with Thomas Newlin in 1891 and extending to the present with Dr. Robin Baker, the institution's 12th president.

In this long line of chief executives, Levi T. Pennington (1875-1975) deserves our special attention, not only for his longevity at the school, but the extraordinary national reputation he built for himself and his college without the benefit of computers, e-mail, cell phones, television or airplanes. It was done with sheer intellect and the force of his personality, during a time of world war and the worst depression this country has ever known.

Throughout his long and productive life of 99 years, 30 of which he spent at GFU when it was known as Pacific College (1911-1941), he was always writing, which helps explain the mechanism he used to become so well respected by so many around the world.

Said his biographer, Donald McNichols, in 1980: "He left behind three book-length unpublished manuscripts and more than 100,000 letters. He was active in every field of endeavor involving his church and college, including education, the ministry, fundraising, evangelism, temperance, peace, war, relief, and politics. In these pursuits he gave countless addresses and sermons (all across America), wrote hundreds of reports, news stories and articles, penned more than three volumes of poetry, wrote an autobiography and kept a diary."

Pennington was born Aug. 29, 1875, in a log cabin near Amo, Ind., the sixth in a family of 10 children, five boys and five girls. His parents were Quaker, his father a country store proprietor, farmer and pastor of the Friends meeting in Manton, Mich.

He completed high school in Manton, worked for a time as a newspaper reporter and city editor, married Bertha May Waters in 1898 and fathered two daughters. In 1903, his world was shattered when he lost Bertha. That same year he answered the call to follow in his father's footsteps and become a Quaker minister.

In 1905, he married Florence Rebecca Kidd and they would remain partners for the rest of their lives, residing while in Newberg at 1000 Sheridan Street. Today, their home is the headquarters of the George Fox University Alumni Association.

Pennington graduated from Earlham College in Richmond, Ind., in 1910.

In 1911, he accepted the presidency at Pacific College. He was 35 years old and would stay in the position until 1941, retiring at age 66.

As we learned in a previous story, Pennington took over from Acting President William Reagan, who had served for a year and who warned his replacement the job would not always be easy. "It has been unusually hard to make ends meet," Reagan said, "and we are about 3 months behind on salaries. You will be head janitor of the institution and the head janitor gets to do all the extras."

He immediately announced a campaign to build an endowment for the college. The goal was set at $100,000, achieved on New Year's Eve, 1914. In 1925, the fund reached $200,000. In doing so, the college received full accreditation from the Bureau of Education.

When news reached the campus, classes were cancelled, the old bell in the Academy building rang out, and faculty and students marched through town in celebration.

During World War I, Pennington stayed true to his Quaker beliefs and remained opposed to the war. Pacific was the only college in Oregon to teach courses in German and also refused to institute programs to train soldiers. However, 25 male students left for France to provide humanitarian service as conscientious objectors.

He also valued athletics. In 1912, intercollegiate competition became available for women. The program was expanded in 1917 and again in 1922. In 1916, he supported an expansion of the school's gymnasium, built by students who had spliced two barns together 21 years earlier.

In 1939, he supervised a major overhaul of Kanyon Hall (now Minthorn Hall).

Pennington and Herbert Hoover were longtime friends and would spend time together on the rare occasions the former U.S. president had a chance to return to Newberg. It is a well-known fact of local history (but worth repeating here) that Hoover spent much of his boyhood years growing up in Newberg while living with his aunt and uncle, John and Laura Minthorn.

In 1954, Pennington received an invitation from Stanford University to speak at the commencement marking the 50th anniversary of the university, during which Hoover was to be given an honorary doctorate.

Hoover and Pennington were fishing partners. Levi and Rebecca were often guests of Mr. Hoover at his suit in the Waldorf Towers in New York City. The Penningtons would usually combine this with visits to Greene, N.Y., to see their daughter, Mary Pearson, and her family.

On Oct. 22, 1964, he gave the sermon at a special service at Friends Church in Newberg eulogizing Herbert Hoover to honor the former president's passing. It was held at the same time as Hoover's memorial service back East. Hoover was, all through life and up to the time of his death, an official member of the church.

He and Rebecca remained in Newberg the rest of their lives, as the former college president remained active in speaking, writing, teaching and participating in activities at Newberg Friends Church. In May 1962, a residence hall honoring the couple was built and is known as Pennington Hall.

Upon the death of Rebecca in 1960, Herbert Hoover sent his friend a heartfelt letter of condolence. ❖

A forgotten tale about Herbert Hoover

Because flooding on the Mississippi River is always a hot news topic, and because Newberg has an important historical connection to flooding on America's largest river through U.S. President Herbert Clark Hoover (1874-1964), let's discuss in this context a seldom-told story about our 31st president that happened back in 1927.

First, a bit of Hoover's background you may already know.

Born in Iowa, the future president came west to Oregon in 1885 as the adopted son of his uncle and aunt, Henry John and Laura Minthorn. The Hoover-Minthorn House at the corner of 2nd and River streets sits in silent testimony to this formative period in young Hoover's life.

His stay in Newberg lasted about four years, from 1885-1889, long enough to give the city its distinction as the only community in the Pacific Northwest to have produced a president of the United States. He attended Friends Pacific Academy (now George Fox University. Aunt Laura taught there and Uncle John was in charge of the school.

Jump ahead to 1927.

In the spring of that year, flooding on the Mississippi River inundated the homes of over 650,000 people. It remains one of the greatest natural disasters this country has ever known.

To get a mental picture of what we're talking about, let's consider for a moment that when the Morganza and Bonnet Carre flood control spillways were opened in 2012 above and below Louisiana's capital city of Baton Rouge, water levels along that stretch of the river had exceeded 1.5 million cubic feet per second.

In 1927, along this same stretch of river, water flow was reported to be *three* million cubic feet per second. Lacking the modern system of levees built during the 1930s, updated with the construction of other flood-control devices during subsequent decades, the river broke through at 145 places in seven states.

The legendary Mounds Landing break 12 miles above Greenville, Miss., sent more than double the water volume of Niagara Falls out on to the Mississippi countryside. In some places the river spread to a width of 80 miles, was over 30-feet deep, with the worst flooding in an area over 100 miles in length. Two hundred forty-six people lost their lives.

In the aftermath, then President Calvin Coolidge began looking around for someone with the experience to conduct the massive job of disaster relief now awaiting the nation. That person was his Secretary of Commerce, Herbert Hoover.

A decade earlier, Hoover had served as food administrator for America during World War I, with vast powers over everything from pricing to distribution. After the war, he ran a European relief program that fed millions.

For the flood, it would now be his job to mobilize state and local authorities, the American Red Cross, the Army Corps of Engineers and others to pull the devastated center of the nation back together.

This he did, for the most part successfully, and one of the high marks of the work would be his skillful use of a grant from the Rockefeller Foundation and other sources of private philanthropy to start public health programs in the hardest hit areas of Louisiana, Arkansas and Mississippi.

These facilities were instrumental in keeping cases of malaria, typhoid fever and vitamin deficiency diseases from breaking out in epidemic numbers. This use of citizen-power provided Hoover a chance to quip, "I suppose I could have called in the Army to help, but why should I, when I only had to call upon Main Street."

For the remainder of the year, Newberg's own was front-page news in every newspaper in the country. Relying on his genius in the emerging field of media-driven image-building and public relations, Hoover used the Flood of 1927 to help launch his bid for the presidency in 1928. He served in the nation's highest office from 1929-1933.

Hoover's treatment of African-Americans after the disaster, *vis-a-vis* his public image as a great humanitarian, remains interesting and controversial among historians. For more on the flood and Hoover's role in it, see John M. Barry's award-winning book, *Rising Tide: The Great Mississippi Flood of 1927 and How It Changed America*, (Simon-Schuster, 1997). Barry delivers an extraordinary treatment of an extraordinary story and talks at length about Hoover's part in it. ❖

When oration ruled

In American society today, nothing on the list of school extracurriculars touches football in levels of attention or prestige.

However, a century ago, at the dawn of Bruin football in 1894, this wasn't the case.

Student life on campus then was much different. At hundreds of institutions across the country, large and small, oration was king. In fact, students skilled in oratory were often more popular than athletes.

And GFU (formerly Pacific College) was not just good at oration, it was great at it, the best in the state of Oregon and in 1904 the best in the United States.

Oration? How could a name for something that sounds like a sleeping pill have been such a big deal?

It was.

In the decades before radio and television, the ability to speak in public, the use of your voice and intelligence to entertain, inform and persuade, was held in very high esteem.

Oration—simply put, speechmaking—was popular enough to be the talk of the town, any town.

Nothing before or since has galvanized Newberg like student speechmaking did in the years before 1910. Pacific College's student orators were local heroes and heroines, admired for their intelligence, persuasiveness and qualities of good character.

From 1893-1907, Pacific placed first four times and second three times in contests sponsored by the State Oratorical Association, a collection of schools that included Oregon Agricultural College (now OSU), the University of Oregon, Willamette University and the Baptist College of McMinnville (now Linfield College).

With each victory, Newberg celebrated in ways that still inspire.

After Elwood Minchin won the state title in 1901, the entire town shut down and proceeded to the train depot on North Main, where folks anxiously awaited the arrival of the young champion and his victory entourage of 60 locals and members of the campus community.

The *Graphic* described it this way:

"A carriage had been appropriately decorated with bunting, a streamer inscribed with 'victory' stretched across the top, and above all a new broom, eloquently expressive of a clean sweep.

"Snatched from the train to the shoulders of his admirers, young Minchin was borne triumphantly to the carriage and thrust into the seat of honor. Eager hands caught the

rope that had been attached to the vehicle and in triumphal procession was started through the streets, accompanied by the blowing of whistles, the ringing of bells and…a fanfare of trumpets of the tin-horn variety."

In 1904, Pacific College scored on the big stage when student Walter Miles won the national contest of the Prohibition Association of Colleges, in what was described by the media as "the greatest oratorical contest between college students that has ever taken place in the United States."

Schools from at least 20 states were represented. Miles was the last to speak and his presentation was described as "electrified by something supernatural."

"Shall we surrender?" he thundered, standing on his tiptoes and glaring at an audience estimated at 4,000.

"No, no," they shouted back.

The whole audience went wild with applause.

A man blasted out, "Another Patrick Henry."

In the 1907 state contest in McMinnville, freshman Katherine Romig Otis railed against sweatshop child labor in the United States in a speech titled, "The Goblin Army." Among the judges were the president of Stanford University and the managing editor of *The Oregonian*.

The *Graphic* reported:

"From the first she had the big audience at perfect command. Her subject itself challenged attention, and as she pictured in burning words the conditions of child labor in America and the dangers with which it threatens our country, as she plead for the overburdened little toilers of the silent, infant army, she carried her hearers with her in sympathy. Her striking climaxes were marked by the thrilling hush which is the tribute to real oratory."

In the audience were over 200 of Newberg's finest, including the entire Pacific College student body of 88. The contingent had chartered a steam train to take them to the Friday night contest. Her opponents were "large men and further along in college." Everyone had arrived at the auditorium and had "made the house ring with songs and yells."

Returning to Newberg with the top prize, a rousing cheer went up from a crowd of waiting admirers. A six-horse team drove Katherine down First Street to the campus. That Sunday, she repeated her winning performance to a packed house at Friends Church. ❖

The Crusader Bowl

In the graveyard of gone and forgotten college bowl games, we find two such bowls with strong ties to the state of Oregon. Both date to the same year. On the obscure scale, they are right at the top.

The first is (or was) the Gotham Bowl, featuring OSU when it was still known as Oregon State College.

It was to be played in Yankee Stadium on Dec. 10, 1960. When numerous attempts to find an opponent for the Beavers failed, the game was scrapped at the last minute and the Corvallis lads stayed home. (Note: For the record, the Gotham Bowl was contested for the 1961 and 1962 seasons before lack of big-money sponsors did it in.)

The second is even more obscure. It had a life span of only one year, also in 1960, and it involved our very own George Fox University, known then as George Fox College.

Yes, George Fox once played football at the collegiate level. The first collegiate home game was against Willamette University on Dec. 1, 1894, in which the Quakers ended up on the short end of a 16-0 score.

From that point on, including a number of times in which the sport was discontinued and then reinstated, football at the school held on until it was permanently discontinued after the 1968 season. From that last team, Bob Hadlock was drafted by the Detroit Lions of the NFL.

There were many lean years during the long period of GFU football, but 1960 turned out to be a good one.

The season started with a bang; four initial wins had everyone in Newberg buzzing. Unfortunately, injuries and grades reduced the program to 21 participants, forcing a final 4-3 record. The players packed everything up and prepared to complete the term.

Our story moves to Los Angeles.

Gil Rinard, 1960 team captain, now a retired Emory University professor living in McMinnville, recalls what happened next.

"The head football coach (name not known) at Los Angeles Pacific College was a great self-promoter, so he came up with the idea of a bowl game that would help promote Christian colleges. He called it the Crusader Bowl."

The home team would be his team. For an opponent, he looked north to Oregon and George Fox College.

Steve Wilhite, Rinard's teammate and a well-known surgeon in Eugene, said the invitation came as a surprise.

"The problem was, we had done quite well until mid-season, then we lost some really good players. We lost our quarterback and the guy he threw the ball to, and they were a very good passing combination. We didn't feel our record was good enough to go to a bowl. However, when the invitation came, we said, 'Sure, let's go.' "

Realizing the Crusader Bowl would give his college unprecedented exposure in one of the nation's largest cities, GFC President Milo Ross decided to expand on the idea by scheduling the college's a cappella choir on a tour of southern California.

He also found a basketball tournament, the Pacific New Year's Basketball Tournament on Jan. 3, willing to accept the Quakers.

With total enrollment that fall at 179, double-duty student involvement was normal, meaning that seven members of the football team were also on the basketball team. There were even a few footballers who sang in the choir. The trip was made by a single bus with enough seating to handle all three groups.

If the trip did much to promote the Newberg college, it did little to promote Quaker football. Played at Occidental College's football stadium on Saturday, Dec. 31, 1960, Los Angeles Pacific defeated George Fox 28-0, in a game tied 0-0 at half. Official attendance was listed at 1,000.

In the third quarter, after recovering a fumble on the Quaker 38-yard line, LAPC completed a 30-yard pass for a touchdown and the rout was on. The final touchdown came on a 63-yard fake kick play on fourth down.

Dr. Wilhite said the lack of players finally wore everyone to a frazzle. "We were tired beyond belief. I was in the game almost every down at several positions." Asked what it felt like to play before such a large crowd, he said it was a lot of fun. Crowds back in Newberg he described as, "Multiply the mothers by three."

Of interest to our story is the fact that the University of Minnesota's marching band attended the game. They were in town for the 1961 Rose Bowl, featuring the University of Washington and their own Golden Gophers, ranked No. 1 in the country at the time. The Minnesota musicians entertained the delighted Crusader Bowl crowd at halftime, using the opportunity to practice their Rose Bowl show. One wonders if this might not be unique in the annals of college football. ❖

WAR STORIES

When Billy Yank came marching West

It wasn't the rattle of musketry, or disease, or blasts from 12-pound Napoleon cannons that did Henry Hopkins in during his years of soldiering in the Civil War.

It was a passion for fife and drum music that killed the ancient veteran.

In 1944, Hopkins, who lived here in town with his daughter on College Street, was Oregon's oldest Civil War veteran.

Several days before a March 3 birthday that would put him three years shy of a century, he had performed two concerts in Newberg, at the high school and on First Street.

His band mate that day was 95-year-old veteran Theodore A. Penland of Portland.

They would often get together to play favorites from the war, once-popular ditties such as "Yankee Doodle Dandy," "The Girl I Left Behind," the immortal "Battle Hymn of the Republic," and Penland's favorite, "Tenting on the Old Camp Ground."

From the exposure, Hopkins developed pneumonia, from which he never recovered. He died March 29 at age 97.

Today, he sleeps the eternal sleep in the Grand Army of the Republic (GAR) section of Newberg's Friends Cemetery, along with over 100 other Union soldiers who represent at least a fourth of the 377 veterans buried throughout the various sections of the cemetery.

The Grand Army of the Republic was a fraternal organization for soldiers and sailors who had defended America during the Civil War (1861-1865). It was, for that generation, what the American Legion has been for veterans serving since World War I.

Founded in 1866 in Decatur, Ill., the GAR survived until the death of the last Civil War veteran in 1956. Its peak membership came in 1890 with over 490,000 members.

The GAR was organized into "Departments" at the state level and "Posts" at the local level. Newberg was home to Post 77.

The social event of the year was the "encampment." The first national encampment was held in 1866 and the last in 1949.

Here in Newberg, encampments were usually held on July 4. It is from this annual tradition that we can loosely trace the origins of today's Old Fashioned Festival.

Presumably, other local GAR legacies include street names honoring prominent Union Civil War generals: Grant, Sheridan, Sherman.

In addition, 40 percent of all Union soldiers who eventually settled in this part of the county were from regiments assigned to the state of Illinois. Thus, we have East and West Illinois streets, formerly just Illinois Street, the only byway in Newberg named for a state.

Other regiments served belonged to Indiana, Iowa, Michigan, Minnesota, New York, Ohio and Wisconsin.

It is fascinating to note that Mr. Penland was the last national commander-in-chief of the GAR, having been appointed to the post *in perpetuity* in 1949 at the organization's final encampment.

At the time, this former veteran of the 152nd Indiana was 100 years old and one of only eight surviving Union veterans of the war. He had used the Emigrant Trail to come west in 1868, had then helped build the Transcontinental Railroad.

Penland is buried at Portland's Memorial Mausoleum.

On May 5, 1868, then GAR Commander-in-Chief General John A. Logan established May 30 as "Decoration Day," which has since become Memorial Day, the GAR's most enduring legacy.

Evidence suggests Logan may have gotten his idea from the ladies of the South, who were honoring the graves of their war dead as early as 1864. A hymn composed by Nella L. Sweet and published in 1867, "Kneel Where Our Loves Are Sleeping," is dedicated to "The Ladies of the South who are Decorating the Graves of the Confederate Dead."

Newberg's GAR section of the Friends Cemetery dates to May 18, 1892. A sign at the entrance mentions the "Kilpatrick Post" as the responsible organization.

This is interesting because the website, *The Grand Army of the Republic and Kindred Societies: Department of Oregon Post Names and Locations*, sponsored by the Library of Congress, lists GAR Post No. 77 in Newberg as the Shiloh Post. Though most of our Civil War veterans are buried here, others can be found scattered throughout the cemetery at large.

Sample interments:

N.E. Britt: A native of New York, he was born in 1843 and died in Newberg in 1927 at age 84. Britt lived in Newberg for 39 years and was very prominent around town, where he was known as the "Father of the Filbert Industry." He served in two volunteer New York regiments, the last of which was cavalry assigned to General Philip Sheridan's Shenandoah Valley campaign in 1864.

James M. Lewelling: A member of the 22nd Indiana Infantry Regiment, Lewelling was reportedly the last surviving member of the honor guard that watched over Abraham Lincoln's body while he lay in state at the Indiana state house in Indianapolis, April 30, 1865. The scheduled stopover was part of the route Lincoln's funeral train took to Springfield, Ill., for burial. Over 100,000 visitors filed past the casket, many standing in the rain for an hour or more for a chance to pay their last respects. Lewelling was born in 1841 and died in 1935.

Henry John Minthorn: He served in the 44th Infantry Regiment, state of Iowa. Minthorn was born in Canada in 1846 and was President Herbert Hoover's uncle and foster father. He died in 1922. Minthorn took part in the latter stages of the war as rear guard support for General Sherman's Atlanta campaign.

John W. Moore: Born in Pennsylvania in 1842, Moore fought with the 18th Wisconsin infantry and served the entire war, with engagements at Shiloh, Chattanooga and Sherman's march through Georgia. He moved to Newberg in 1902 and died 21 years later.

At least one veteran buried at Friends, **Sam Edward Lewellen**, was a Confederate, enrolled under the command of General Sterling Price in Missouri. ❖

"No place for a mother's son"

It is now forgotten by most that Veterans Day owes its origins to a war now forgotten by most: World War I, known at the time as "The Great War" or "The War to End All Wars."

It was officially over with the signing of the Treaty of Versailles on June 28, 1919. However, fighting had ceased seven months earlier thanks to an armistice called by the Allied nations and Germany and which became effective at the 11th hour of the 11th day of the 11th month of the year 1918.

In November 1919, President Woodrow Wilson proclaimed Nov. 11 as "Armistice Day." Congress approved the date as a legal holiday in 1938. In June 1954, Congress substituted the word "armistice" with "veterans" and established Nov. 11 as a day to honor American veterans of all wars.

The Great War was a colossal event spanning five years, involving 26 major countries and costing the lives of 17 million soldiers and civilians, including 116,000 from the United States after this country entered the fray on April 6, 1917.

This was also the first war covered by *The Newberg Graphic* in detail. Editions of the paper carried letters from the front written by locals.

One of the most chilling was penned by Dave Smith to his girl friend, Inez Dodge, in August 1917.

Smith, a former employee at the town bakery, was so anxious to rid the world of the German threat he had joined the Canadian army 13 months before America entered the war. At the time, he was in a hospital in Essex County, England, convalescing with a knee wound.

"My brother was out here 29 months and was wounded three times before he was killed. I had a long talk with him a month before he got it, it being the first time I had seen him in nine years and I certainly had a fine time with him. I met him in the trenches. Arlie Evans wrote me a very nice letter and by the way it read he must be very anxious to come out here. I answered his letter and told him not to be in too big a hurry for he would not be here long before he wished he was back in Newberg, for I have wished it many a time. This is no place for a mother's son and another thing, they kill out here."

Newberg, of course, was not like most other towns, not when it came to *war*.

Home to one of the largest communities of the Society of Friends in the western United States, Quakers had followed a doctrine of witnessing for peace since the year 1660. It's easy to understand how The "Grubby End" could have had a pacifist image among neighboring towns in the Willamette Valley, which, in the tense and uncertain atmosphere of a country that had just committed itself to a world war and might be interpreted by some as unpatriotic. Quakerism, to anyone with little or no knowledge of the denomination, was a tempting target for unfounded prejudices and silly notions about subversive behavior.

No one knew this better than Pacific College (now GFU) President Levi Pennington who, on April 19, 1917, had to ask for his own space in *The Graphic* to squash a "rumor" meant to imply sedition. This one involved a student who reportedly had ripped an American flag from the dress of a fellow student and had thrown it on the floor.

Said Pennington on what actually did happen:

"The only incident that has occurred remotely resembling it is the following, according to those who saw and participated in the affair. One of the young women of the student body took a flag from the dress of one of her best girlfriends, purely in the spirit of mischief, and just as other students had done before they realized that the flag is not a fit subject for playfulness. No indignity was offered the flag, which was later returned to its owner."

At the same time, Pennington refused an offer to institute an ROTC program on campus for the training of military officers, saying his decision correlated with Jesus' and Quaker tradition.

Twenty-five Pacific students went to Europe and helped the war effort through food production and conservation work. Alumnus Herbert Hoover, one day to be U.S. president, was known as "America's famous food commissioner" for his work in heading up relief efforts in Europe for the war's displaced civilians.

So, what was Newberg really like during the Great War? A nest of peace lovers who refused to do anything for the country in its time of crisis? Or a town of patriots?

The answer is the city did its duty.

Anticipating something big was about to happen, on Friday, March 30, a week before Wilson's declaration, Mayor Larkin issued a call for the town to conduct a "patriotic meeting" at Duncan's Hall, a popular gathering place in town for such events.

The response was overwhelming, the crowd swamping the seating capacity of the building. Patriotic speeches were given by the Rev. George H. Lee and headliner Judge John H. Stevenson of Portland. The judge urged all to conduct themselves with cool judgment and to give President Wilson full support "if the worst should come." When he sat down, surrounded by a stage full of Civil War veterans, everyone joined together in the singing of "national airs" to the music of Kienle's Orchestra.

By July 5 over 4,100 Oregonians had volunteered, in the vernacular of the time, to "fight the Hun." Almost 150 of these were from Yamhill County. Another 167 were credited to neighboring Polk. Newberg's population was around 2,500.

One man who wanted to enlist was "Uncle" John Dowd, Jr., age 105.

Still able to walk two miles a day, and a veteran of the Civil and Indian wars, Uncle John said, "it was not age but the size of the fight in the dog that mattered."

For 13 local men, the trip to the trenches was forever. Only World War II had more war-related deaths.

Their names are enshrined in Memorial Park as a lasting tribute to their sacrifices: William B. Burnham, Alvin T. Graves, Melvin S. Iverson, Charles W. Jensen, Dale Melrose, Elmer A. Mills, John Pettengill, Lester C. Rees, Irvin M. Swart, Bert H. Udell, Herman Vanderbeck, Lloyd Whitmore and Richard P. Youngs.

Newberg's American Legion Post 57 is named in Rees' honor. Read more about him in the story, "Let us never forget" in this section. ❖

Newberg's day of infamy

Maybe you were alive at the time and still remember. Or you've heard about it from others, or read about it, or seen film or photos of it on TV, the fire and smoke pouring from the twisted metal of what was once the U.S. Navy's mighty Pacific fleet, the sheer panic in the faces of the people, the images of a nation stunned and in pain.

No matter how you know about this defining moment in American history, Dec. 7, 1941 is the day President Franklin Delano Roosevelt said would "live in infamy," the day America, through the Japanese attack on Pearl Harbor, Hawaii, was finally forced into World War II.

The story of how Newberg reacted to the attack has never been told anywhere (except in newspaper reporting at the time), so let's do it now, as we pay tribute to a date on the calendar that should never be forgotten.

The year 1941 had been good to Newberg, with great progress shown after a miserable decade of the 1930s and the Great Depression.

Building permits were up from 1940, the Chamber of Commerce was energized (under the direction of new president E.L. Morton) and on a campaign to attract industry to the area. There was talk of an airport and planning got under way to make it happen.

Enrollments in the public schools were climbing. Pacific College named Emmett Gulley to replace a retiring Levi Pennington as its new president. Under Gulley, the small Quaker college would experience historic growth in enrollment and in its physical plant.

New street lights made nights around downtown a bit easier to maneuver. A new maraschino cherry unit was opened at the Allen Fruit cannery. Teachers at the high school got raises and Yamhill County announced that for the first time since 1919, it would pay for what it needed with cash.

It was a peaceful time. But it was a nervous and jittery peace.

The news from around the world was full of conflict, with folks wondering how long it would be before America was forced to weigh in with something other than political rhetoric. On the local scene, there were signs that things were not right, that a bit of advanced preparation might be a helpful thing.

How else to explain the formation on June 19 of a Yamhill County Defense Council to coordinate what it simply referred to as "activities"

Or the stiffening of penalties for draft dodgers?

Had anyone noticed that the town's longtime National Guard unit, Battery F of the 218th Field Artillery Battalion, was away for training of such duration that it was granted a three-day furlough on July 8 so the men could see their families? The moniker "weekend warrior" had suddenly taken on a whole new meaning.

And what about the Boy Scouts collecting scrap metal for the military? Or the Rotary and Chamber inviting military personnel to address their gatherings?

Was it true the state was going to build a defense training facility in Newberg and that instruction would be free? And what about the Yamhill Army Group, an organization for young boys much like the junior ROTC programs at Oregon public schools, the latter enjoying its best membership since 1918.

Who suspected something might not be right when Newberg took part in a nationwide test of a blackout on Oct. 31? It lasted three and one-half minutes and cost the city council $14,404.50, a sum which they gladly paid.

Whatever the suspicions, Newberg's world, along with the rest of America, changed with Pearl Harbor. The surprise attack left 2,388 civilian and military dead, 1,178 wounded, and eliminated the U.S. Pacific fleet as an effective fighting force. It shocked the town and left people feeling numb and betrayed.

As soon as word of the attack reached the city, Newberg began its own version of mobilizing for war. Rumors were everywhere, with understandable attendant fear that the Japanese were about to land on the Oregon coast.

Putting the call out that the town needed a home defense unit, the Newberg fire department coordinated a gathering of over 300 of the well-intentioned at city hall. The group included many veterans of World War I, now ready to serve their country once again. Overwhelming the space, they adjourned to the Legion hall, where Carl Butler, a former Army captain, was appointed executive officer.

Armed with bird guns, shotguns and everything in between, some of the men had managed to squeeze into old uniforms or various other articles of military clothing. Organizing into six groups of approximately 25 men each and referring to themselves as the "Minutemen," these citizen soldiers began guarding the bridges on opposite ends of the town and patrolling the streets, being especially on the lookout for anything suspicious at or near the town's water supply.

When the rumored attack did not materialize (about two days later) Mayor George Layman thanked everyone and turned over their "duties" to the sheriff's department.

The atmosphere was pure patriotism; everybody wanted to do something, anything to help. The folks living out in West Chehalem came up with the novel idea that in case of attack, a makeshift air raid alarm of car horns would let everyone know. On Jan. 1, 1942, the system was tested.

As agreed to at a community meeting at the Ewing Young school auditorium, Alvin Smith, Adolf Wohlgemuth, Rudolph Leffler, Kenneth Fendall, Al Boyd, Bill Dopp, Harvey Davis, Henry Hiedeman, Frank Brian and Harvey Nelson were all supposed to blow their horns at the appointed hour, which would then trigger other activities in the community to ready the neighborhood to meet the enemy.

The hour came…and went…with a single horn heard. In the *Graphic*, an unnamed "correspondent" reported the following:

"Your correspondent is admirably situated to hear signals from many directions but heard only the horn of Rudolf Leffler, and our own family did not even hear the horn on the family car, though blown vociferously for 10 to 15 seconds. Reports from other listeners corroborated our findings locally. Obviously some other plan will have to be devised when the next civilian defense meeting is held. Watch this column for announcements…."

It was also at the start of 1942 that war-related announcements began to hit the *Graphic* with such frequency that the newspaper became like a giant bulletin board for what was expected of Americans at war.

Farmers were notified by the Army that all horses and mules, age 3-10, had to be registered by Jan. 10. In a story that would be a harbinger of how life was going to be over the next five years, Yamhill County officials announced the appointment by Oregon Governor Sprague of a Tire and Automobile Rationing Committee, comprised of prominent local citizens H.M. Washbond and educator Antonia Crater.

In support of the new program, Newberg Police Chief Art Casteel encouraged car owners to register their tires. "You can't buy 'um, so folks are gonna steal 'um," he said. The Berrian Service Station, Palmer's Garage and the Dayton Garage were designated as tire inspection stations. It was their responsibility to say "yea" or "nay" to drivers needing new rubber.

Over the next two weeks, reading the *Graphic* was a small-world experience for folks who felt they were a million miles from the action. Maybe in distance, but not in lives.

Among the Pearl Harbor dead were three young men with Newberg connections.

The first was James Milton Robertson, a machinist mate first class aboard *USS Arizona*. He was a nephew of Mrs. A.A. Anderson of Rt. 1, Newberg.

The second was Harvey George Rushford, 18, a seaman second class stationed on *USS Nevada* and one of the 50 aboard the giant battleship that fateful day killed in action. He was the son of Mrs. Fred Bryant of Newberg, who had five sons in the service at the time of the attack. She told the *Graphic*: "Even if I had 15 sons, I would gladly give them all to the service."

Clair Clifton Myers, killed aboard *USS West Virginia*, had a brother, Martin Myers, who worked at Nap's grocery.

Finally, Edward Davis lost his life aboard battleship *USS California*.

Pearl Harbor reached out and touched Newberg in numerous other ways as well, with the men and women living and working *there* who had either grown up here, lived here at some point in their lives, or had relatives who did. All witnessed the events of Dec. 7.

From Newberg:

Bruce Rogers was in Tokyo with the U.S. Embassy diplomatic staff at the time of the attack. He was housed at a Tokyo hotel waiting for passports and permission to leave country.

Paul Cookingham, a member of the Willamette University football team, was in Honolulu at the time of the attack, having just finished a game the night before with the University of Hawaii.

Mrs. J.T. Watson and her husband were living in Honolulu, where he was an electrician.

Lee Switzer was a Navy pilot.

Raymond Hornibrook served aboard *USS New Orleans*.

Thomas Mountain, a Newberg teacher for many years, had just moved to Hawaii.

Stationed at Pearl Harbor was Captain Robert DuPriest, a medical doctor. ❖

The dead of World War II

Ploesti.

During World War II, this was the name given to the complex of refineries north of Bucharest, Romania, responsible for 60 percent of the refined oil necessary to keep the German war machine operating.

Called "the taproot of German might" by English Prime Minister Winston Churchill, Ploesti was a prized Allied target hit numerous times during the war.

No attack, however, carried higher expectations than the one launched on "Black Sunday," Aug. 1, 1943. One hundred seventy-eight B-24 Liberator bombers were sent from bases in North Africa and assigned to annihilate Ploesti, a round-trip distance of 2,000 miles. Fifty-three would not return.

Aboard one of the bombers was Newberg's Alfred M. Zielaskowski, a sergeant in the U.S. Army Air Corps. During the war he was awarded the Silver Star, the Distinguished Flying Cross and the Air Medal with oak leaf cluster. He remains one of Newberg's most decorated servicemen from any war. How he won his Silver Star is an extraordinary story of courage and determination.

Arriving at the target, the Allied bombers were confronted by one of the most heavily protected facilities in the German arsenal.

It was surrounded by hundreds of anti-aircraft guns, terrifying to flyers because of the thick clouds of exploding shells (known as flak) they could throw into the sky, and which could easily penetrate a plane's fuselage and turn the interior into a killing zone.

Ploesti's protective shield included a specially designed flak train, whose sides could be dropped to reveal batteries of artillery racing along the tracks in tandem with attacking aircraft.

Whether it was the train or some other set of guns that hit Alfred's plane, we will never know. What we do know is that flak delivered his Liberator a potentially fatal blow; hydraulic lines responsible for keeping the craft aloft were seriously damaged and needed immediate attention.

Also, when the plane was hit, the bomb bay doors were open—the bombs had just been dropped—and now they wouldn't close. A catwalk slippery with oil and gasoline traversed this exposed section of the plane's belly. Below was nothing but the ground thousands of feet below. The hydraulic lines in question ran through this open space. To get to them, someone would have to crawl along the catwalk, where the slightest mishap would drop a man beneath and away from the plane and into eternity.

Sgt. Zielaskowski volunteered to be that guy. Still over the target, he left his station as top turret gunner, repaired the lines and helped his plane return to an emergency landing in Sicily. Surviving, Ploesti, he was reported missing in action after another raid to Romania two weeks later.

Of the 41 other names we have of Newberg's dead of World War II, some died in places like Hawaii, Tunisia, Okinawa, Italy and the Philippines, while others never made it to the front. Instead, they were lost in training accidents or to disease. In two cases, all they did was something as simple as cross the street.

Here's a sampling:

Donald Wendall Adams, who lived on Sheridan Street, was listed as missing in action in the Pacific on June 6, 1945.

When war broke out, **William Binshadler** was the assistant manager of the JC Penny store on E. First. He was killed when the munitions depot where he was stationed was bombed.

John Haworth died Jan. 21, 1944, on a training mission in Corpus Christi, Texas. He was an instructor at the naval air station.

A similar fate befell **C. Frank Brooks**, a gunner aboard a B-17 that went down 77 miles north of Memphis, Tenn. All hands aboard were killed. Brooks owned a print shop he had bought from his father in downtown Newberg in 1940. He was a popular member of the Rotary and the Chamber of Commerce.

Ralph Lehmann died in Italy on Feb. 3, 1944. He was 20 years old and had been president of the Future Farmers of America at Newberg Union High, where he was also a member of the debate team. A forward observer for his artillery unit, Lehmann was awarded the Silver Star for gallantry, beginning when he carried a radio transmitter 150 yards over open ground under intense enemy fire. Hiding in a house, he further exposed himself by holding a radio antenna out of the window in full view of enemy gunners. Shell fragments killed him while he was transmitting a message back to his unit.

William Keller was 25 when he fell beneath the wheels of a trailer truck in New York City. He was born in Romania, was one of 13 children, and had moved with his family from North Dakota to Newberg in 1940.

Murray Landauer died on Okinawa.

Lawrence "Bud" Randall lost his life in the Italian Campaign. His parents owned the Baker Grocery at 9th and Willamette streets. His mother was a cousin to Newberg Mayor R.N. Hutchins.

Frank Schwarzin was a chief electrician's mate and had been in the service for 23 years. Reported as missing in action on April 9, 1945, he lived at 600 2nd Street and left behind a wife and four daughters.

George L. Wright, after whom Newberg's VFW 4015 Post is named, was killed in Tunisia, North Africa, on April 9, 1943. Wright is honored more extensively in the story in this section titled, "Let us never forget." ❖

Let us never forget

The highest honor a community can give a veteran is to name an American Legion or Veterans of Foreign War post after him (or her).

In Newberg, we have both organizations, and the veterans so honored are Lester C. Rees of American Legion Post 57, and George L. Wright of VFW Post 4015.

Rees lost his life during World War I.

Wright was the first from Newberg to die in combat in World War II.

For both, so much time has passed no one today from the active memberships of the local posts remembers them.

In the case of Lester Rees, a marble plate mounted to the top of an old desk at the old VFW Hall on S. Howard (both groups met here until the spring of 2014) shows Oct. 12, 1918, as the day he was killed. It also gives the place: Gesnes, France.

Sadly, this was a mere 29 days short of Armistice Day, Nov. 11, the day the war ended. In 1938, Congress used this same date to establish a permanent holiday to honor veterans and the cause of world peace.

Eighty-five years later, Lester Rees sleeps the eternal sleep at plot A, row 8, grave 19 at the Meuse-Argonne American Cemetery just outside the French village of Romagne, which is quietly tucked away in the region of Lorraine in the northern part of the country.

Gesnes is close by, still a deeply wooded area littered with decaying bunkers and trench lines reminding us this was once the front line of the American Army.

Rees (whose name on his cemetery cross is spelled Reese) shares this lovely spot with 14,246 other American soldiers and sailors. The grounds total 130.5 acres, the largest concentration of American military dead in Europe.

Most of them were lost to us during the Meuse-Argonne Offensive, also known as the Battle of the Argonne Forest. It was fought across the expanse of Lorraine's thick wooded areas and rolling hills from Sept. 26 to Nov. 11, 1918.

This was where Medal of Honor recipient Alvin York made his mark. The same is true of the Lost Battalion. Meuse-Argonne is often called the "bloodiest single battle in American military history."

Rees' cross also indicates he was a mechanic with the Army's 125th Infantry Regiment, 32nd Infantry Division. Many of the men who served with him were from Michigan, and everyone saw heavy combat all during the offensive.

From Oct. 3-13, covering the young man's last week with the unit, the 125th suffered 603 wounded and 173 killed.

In the Newberg Public Library, the oldest copy in the files of the Newberg High School yearbook, *Chehalem,* shows his picture.

He's with a group of friends from the sophomore class. His boyish face is full of wonderment and life, oblivious to the fact that in two years he will be dead beneath the trees of Gesnes, 5,190 miles from home, but a short walk to where he will be laid to rest.

Unlike Rees, the body of George Wright came back to Newberg, where he is with his mother, Arvilla L. Wright, in the GAR section of Friends Cemetery.

Born May 13, 1906, he was 36 years old when he joined the Army. At the time, he had been an employee of the state highway department. There is nothing to indicate he ever married or had children.

A private in the 133rd Infantry Regiment of the 34th Infantry Division, Wright was killed on April 9, 1943, at the Battle for Fondouk Pass in Tunisia, North Africa.

The 133rd had arrived in North Africa from Liverpool, England, on Jan. 3, 1943. The majority of the men were from the state of Iowa.

By Feb. 17, the 133rd was involved in heavy fighting against the 21st Panzer Division of General Erwin Rommel's Afrika Corps.

Later, heavy losses at Kef-el-Amar Pass (March 11) forced the regiment's withdrawal. Time was taken to restock the ranks with replacements, regardless of a man's state of origin. Wright was one of these.

By April 9, they were at Fondouk. The fighting was furious, with attacks launched before sunrise in the pitch black.

On the day he died, Wright and his buddies were instructed to weave toilet paper in their helmet webs so they could see one another during the advance. They rehearsed the sign "grocery" and the countersign "store" as another means of identification. The ration was hardtack and oxtail soup. A slice of white bread was dessert.

A half ton truck was ready in the rear to haul out the dead. The words "The Stuka Valley Hearse" were painted on its side in big white letters.

Ray Fountain, who had worked as a federal bankruptcy arbitrator in Des Moines before the war, commanded the regiment.

As his men prepared to go forward, Fountain walked the ranks giving encouragement. A "tremendous aerial bombing" would soon flatten everything in their front, he said.

The planes never came.

When the war department telegram arrived in Newberg later in April to tell Arvilla her son had been killed in action, it was followed two days later by a cheery letter from George telling her not to worry. ❖

The good ship *SS Newberg*

On February 10, 1944, the Kaiser shipyards at Swan Island in north Portland launched a ship the story of which we shouldn't forget.

Say hello to the *SS Newberg*, a type T-2 oil tanker. Kaiser built over 480 during the years 1943-1945. These ships operated as the workhorses of the tanker fleet during the war, supplying fuel and other vital liquids to ships serving America and its allies around the world.

Watching the "delivery" that day was a large delegation from Newberg which included Mayor R.N. Hutchins, current and past presidents of the Chamber of Commerce, the Newberg Union High School band, and a color guard from the local Boy Scouts.

Once the proceedings were under way, with the giant ship looming overhead, the Rev. John Paxton of the Moreland Presbyterian Church in Milwaukie delivered the blessing.

Finishing, he turned things over to A.R. Nieman, shipyard general manager, who then handed off to the mayor to deliver the main address.

Doing the honors of breaking the bottle across the bow of the ship was *SS Newberg* sponsor, Mrs. Donald H. Sim, wife of the Swan Island assistant master shipwright.

She was accompanied by two matrons of honor and her granddaughter, three-and-a-half-year-old flower girl, Miss Bonnie Allyn Sim.

Miss Caroline Stone sang the lyrics as the high school band played, "When the Lights Go On Again All Over the World."

One of the highlights of the morning was the presentation of a plaque on which was written a brief history of the city of Newberg. This would be the plaque's final stop before making its way to hang inside the captain's cabin aboard ship.

Finally, the ship's crew was toasted by the assembled crowd before M.C. Nieman nodded to Mrs. Sim to put her champagne bottle to good use.

It is uncertain what happened to *SS Newberg* once she entered service.

What is known is that she survived the war and lived on into the 1980s under various other names, including *SS Esso Asheville* (1947), *SS Point Arena* (1960), and *SS Rice Queen* (1964). In 1974, she became a bulk food carrier out of San Francisco.

In 1980, the vessel was converted to a barge and renamed *Delta Conveyor*.

The *SS Newberg* was but one of a number of T-2 tankers given Oregon place names. The records show launchings of *SS The Dalles, SS Crater Lake, SS Pendleton, SS Celilo, SS Tillamook, SS Corvallis, SS Champoeg* and many others.

T-2 tankers were 523 feet long, with a 68-foot beam and a 30-foot draft. Weighing 10,448 tons empty, they were 21,880 tons when fully loaded. The carrying capacity of a T-2 was 141,200 barrels of fuel, which translates to six million gallons.

The 6,000 shaft horsepower Turbo-Electric propulsion plant could push the ship forward to a maximum speed of 16 knots. Crews numbered approximately 50.

During World War II, American tankers made 6,500 voyages to carry 65 million tons of oil and gasoline from the U.S. and the Caribbean to the war zones. They supplied 80 percent of the fuel used by bombers, tanks, jeeps and ships during the war. It was a job well done.

On May 29, 2014, I received an e-mail from Milt Bell, a former crew member of *SS Rice Queen*. He had read my story about the *SS Newberg* in the *Graphic* and wanted to share his memories of what it was like to serve aboard the ship. As you will read, Mr. Bell has lived a most interesting life and comes from a most interesting seafaring family.

"I was born and raised at Port Boca Grande, Fl., which was a deep-water port where phosphate was loaded aboard ships bound for ports around the globe. My father was the port boss and harbor master, and as a result, I had total access to the ships that called.

Rice Queen was a fairly typical T-2 tanker conversion, which was turned into a bulk carrier with all housing aft, (meaning) the midship bridge and officers' quarters were moved aft just forward of the funnel. All her machinery remained the same with the exception of the cargo pumps, which were removed since they were no longer needed. The main propulsion consisted of two steam turbine dynamos, which supplied electricity to a General Electric 6,000hp electric motor which turned the screw. The boilers were one level up from the turbine deck and just aft of the turbines themselves. On the upper level was the steam-drum next to which was a door out into the portside passageway. I hated to use that door because the heat next to that steam-drum was almost unbearable.

During conversion, two of the new improvements to the ship were the installation of central air conditioning and an elevator that traveled from the main deck in the accommodation all the way up to the chartroom. That otherwise would have been about a five or six deck stair climb.

The ship would run about 16 knots under ballast, about 15.5 loaded. She could be a bit of a roller but for the most part I found her to be a good girl. Being on the "ass end" as it were, the pitching and yawing could become tiresome after a while.

When I first became familiar with her, she was carrying rice from Stockton, Calif., to San Juan, PR She would then run empty to my father's port to load phosphate and return to California via the Panama Canal and turn around for the return trip.

I recall one of the mates having given my father a 50-pound sack of rice with the Sello-Rojo logo on it which was also the logo on the ship's funnel. As a young man of 17 and a new Seafarer's International member, I made one trip aboard her as an oiler. I really liked the ship but I had broader horizons and so I started working for Moore-McCormack and United States Lines.

In 2004, I retired from Teco Transport as chief engineer. Oddly enough, my late uncle Joe Bell, who lived in Martinez, Ca., retired as chief engineer aboard Matson Lines SS Lurline *in 1966 and my great-great uncle, a Scotsman named Joseph Bell, was chief engineer aboard* RMS Titanic. *He didn't fare as well."* ❖

Peace Camps

One of the cornerstones George Fox built into his Religious Society of Friends (Quakers) when he founded the movement in the 17th century was something known as the "Peace Testimony."

First discussed in 1651, what he said spoke to the necessity for all Christians to "live in the virtue and power of life which takes away the occasion of war."

In the centuries that have followed, many (though not all) Quakers have used this to justify their refusal to serve in the military during time of war.

This leads to the question of how, then, did Newberg, as one of the principal Quaker communities in the Far West, react to World War II?

Our story begins in 1933 with the Civilian Conservation Corps, a massive, nationwide, quasi-military program launched that year by President Franklin D. Roosevelt for unemployed, unmarried young men between the ages of 18 and 25.

The CCC provided paychecks to workers in desperate need of any kind of job to see them through the lean years of the Great Depression.

In its nine-year life span (1933-42), 2.5 million participated.

Oregon had over 300 of these camps. Enrollees performed a variety of tasks, most of which were forestry-related. Today, Oregonians enjoy the CCC legacy at parks and forests around the state.

Sometime in 1942, as America settled in to World War II, 143 former CCC camps nationwide were converted to accommodate (some would say incarcerate) men opposed to the war, a group often referred to as conscientious objectors, or COs.

Nationally, about 13,000 were so labeled. The sponsorship of these camps was varied, but included the traditional "Peace Churches": United Brethren, Mennonites and Quakers. By the end of the war, these three churches would spend $7 million dollars collectively in supporting peace.

In Oregon, under a federally directed program called Civilian Public Service (CPS), the best-known of these locations included Camp #59 in Elkton (on Highway 38 past Drain on the way to Reedsport), Camp #56, or Camp Angell (just south of Waldport), and a camp located near Cascade Locks in the Columbia River Gorge.

Quakers were especially connected to the Elkton camp. An online source from the Oregon Historical Society states that, "CPS Camp 59…was sponsored by the (American) Friends Service Committee. Work was primarily a continuation of the forest conservation projects started by the CCC, including reforesting cutover lands, road construction, surveying public lands, forest fire prevention, and forest (fire) fighting."

The American Friends Service Committee was headquartered in Philadelphia, Pa. It relied on the Peace Department of the Oregon Yearly Meeting of the Friends Church in Newberg to help coordinate activities in the region associated with CO camps.

The department's superintendent was none other than Levi Pennington, who had retired from a 30-year stint as president of Pacific College (George Fox University) at the close of the 1940-41 school year.

At the June 1942 Yearly Meeting, Pennington reported, "The year…has been marked by America's entrance into the World War. Most pressing among the immediate concerns of the Friends of Oregon Yearly Meeting has been the need to support our young men who have taken their stand as conscientious objectors… and have therefore been assigned to work of national importance under civilian direction."

Outlining the accomplishments of his department, he said: "Many special projects have been carried on by local committees, such as…the furnishing of books for men in the Civilian Public Service Camps…advisory committees for conscientious objectors…work with the National Council for Prevention of War…and the planning of a special class for boys and girls to study and receive instruction…on the subject of peace."

The archives at GFU contains numerous letters in its collection from Quakers assigned to Oregon's CO camps.

Typical of these is one from Melvin Kenworth, who in June 1943 was transferred to the Friends camp in Elkton. "On June 10, I was transported to Big Creek, a side camp of Elkton. The main project was the building of a logging road in order to salvage timber…in the Smith River area. Most of the time (we) spent keeping the camp supplied with firewood."

It must also be said that most Quaker young men during the war decided to join the military. Pennington acknowledged that, by 1942, 23 members had enlisted in combatant military service, with six serving in non-combatant roles.

Quaker Wilford L. Moorman was a storekeeper aboard battleship *USS Iowa*. On July 4, 1944, he wrote, "I have only been away two years, but it seems like 10. We observed the holiday with roast turkey and all the trimmings, plus apple pie and ice cream."

He and his shipmates had earned it. They had just repelled four massive attacks by suicide planes at the Battle of the Philippine Sea and would soon be on their way to help support the landings at Peleliu. ❖

Vietnam War hero Dick Whitney

From his photo in the Newberg High School yearbook, Dick Whitney's face looks straight at you 49 years later with a grin as wide as Nebraska, his father's ancestral home.

In the list of his activities next to his picture, you learn he had participated in Tiger sports, but not his senior year.

That year, 1964, he had devoted his time to Thespians. He was also the vice president of his home room class and had served on the staff of the student newspaper, *Echoes*. An avid outdoorsman, he was a four-year member of the NHS Rod and Gun Club.

Away from school, on July 16, 1962, his 16th birthday, he had soloed in his dad's plane, thus becoming one of Oregon's youngest pilots of the 1960s.

And yet, in spite of all these achievements, nothing about this young man suggests what would become of him over the next five years.

Among the city's war dead honored each Memorial Day, Dick Whitney is one of seven sons of Newberg who never returned from the Vietnam War.

The others, in alphabetical order are David J. Berry, Lester E. Brown, Edward H. Johnson, Michael C. Kamph, Robert Schoen and Ronald Storey.

For the record, at least three others from this list join Dick Whitney as having graduated from NHS, all around the mid-1960s. Kamph was Newberg's first Vietnam casualty, killed by mine fragments Aug. 21, 1967. He was a member of one of the world's top jungle fighting units, the Army's elite 14th Infantry Regiment.

In addition to being a member of this exclusive fraternity of American military heroes, Dick Whitney also holds the distinction of being one of Newberg's most decorated combat soldiers.

In the just shy of 13 total months he served in the Army (May 7, 1968 to May 28, 1969) he would earn the Silver Star, two Bronze stars, a Purple Heart, the Army Commendation Medal with "V" (for valor), a Combat Infantryman's Badge and a host of other medals and ribbons. The Silver Star is the third highest military medal given by this country.

That he would be licensed to fly at such a young age was a given. His father and mother, Sam and Claire Whitney, owned Sportsman Airpark, where Sam was one of the most respected flying instructors in the Pacific Northwest.

As a young man, Sam had moved to Yamhill County with his parents in 1937. Originating in Fullerton, Neb., where he was born and raised and where he had graduated from high school, the Whitneys had given up trying to farm the Great Plains and had opted for the better opportunities afforded by Oregon's Willamette Valley.

They chose the Dayton area to start again and purchased the farm of John and Alda Metcalf Stilwell, one of Yamhill County's most prominent families of pioneer lineage.

In 1939, Sam married John and Alda's daughter, Claire. Graduating from Oregon State College in 1941 with a degree in fish and wildlife management, he learned to fly and then enlisted in the Navy, serving the last two years of the war as a flight instructor in Pensacola, Fla.

Returning home in late 1945, he borrowed $3,000 from his mother-in-law, moved to Newberg and by March 1946 had constructed a dirt runway where the current Airpark runway is today.

Here he would spend the rest of his life teaching others how to fly, helping seed the lakes of Oregon from the air with fish stock for the U.S. Fish and Wildlife Commission, and selling and servicing aircraft, especially planes made by the Piper aircraft company.

In addition to Dick, Sam and Claire also parented a daughter named Lessie, the older of the two siblings. Today, she and husband Jerry Dale own and operate the Airpark.

In a recent interview for this story, Lessie remembered something about her brother that helps explain why he accomplished so much in the less than 23 years he was alive.

"He had more energy than anyone else," she shared. "He was hyperactive, always laughing and having a good time."

Out of high school and much to his father's chagrin, Dick enrolled at the University of Oregon. Lessie says her brother didn't like the UO because it was too big. "So he went to the city and enrolled at Portland State.

"From PSU he was drafted, but he wasn't very happy about it. It was Dad who encouraged him to go in and I guess it's because Dad didn't have any negative feelings about the war. However, Dick really didn't want to go to Vietnam."

After basic training at Ft. Lewis, Wash., Vietnam was exactly where Dick was sent, arriving there in October 1968 as a radio operator in Co. E of the 5th Battalion of the 60th Infantry Regiment.

If it is true he didn't want to go, he never showed it. Over the next seven months, he would experience heavy fighting and begin racking up an impressive combat record for someone so young and inexperienced and who had only been out of boot camp for a few months.

Medals for valor, of which we've already mentioned Dick had three, are always accompanied with written citations describing the conditions under which the awards were given. Lessie says if the family ever had copies they are long gone. All she knows is that her brother died a "hero's death."

There are some details, however, about Dick's last day alive, these from the Oregon National Guard. He had been part of a helicopter-borne reconnaissance platoon in the Mekong Delta region shot at by an enemy combatant who had then fled to a nearby house.

The platoon went in pursuit. Approaching the structure, they immediately realized it was a Viet Cong machine gun nest.

Suddenly, a bullet slammed into Dick. But he continued to fight. Just before he died, he was able to throw a grenade through a window of the house and put the nest out of action. This allowed the rest of the platoon to escape.

In addition to his parents and sister, Dick left behind a wife named Carol, who he had married six months before entering the service, and Carol's 3 ½-year-old daughter, who he had adopted right after the ceremony.

"When he left for the war, there was a lot of anxiety," Lessie adds, "We were devastated when we found out he had been killed. It was very hard on our family."

All these years later, she remains proud of her brother, just as she knows her parents were proud of him during the rest of their lives (both are now deceased).

She concludes: "He was a brave American who put his fear to one side and fought for his country. What could be better than that?"

What indeed. ❖

CELEBRATING NEWBERG

The meaning of "Chehalem"

Over the years, the Newberg Public Library has been blessed with many excellent librarians. One of my favorites, for reasons you are about to learn, was Jennie Miller.

As we saw in the opening story, Ms. Miller lived in Yamhill County for 60 years and died in 1957 at age 93. Her tenure as head librarian spanned the years 1920-1945.

She was born in the state of Maine and moved to Oregon with her parents when she was in the eighth grade.

Her unpublished manuscript, *A History of Newberg: Compiled from facts gathered by Miss Jennie D. Miller 1936-1937-1938*, remains the most in-depth historical snapshot of our city ever done. It's a treasure trove of institutional memory now all but gone.

Copies of her 133-page, typewritten history are rare and considered an absolute must-read for anyone wanting a better understanding of Newberg in the decades before World War II. The next time you're at our library, ask the reference librarian to see the copy on file in the Newberg Collection.

It is from Ms. Miller that we get the first of several meanings for the word "Chehalem," in which she recounts a legend that "Chehalem" was a great Indian chief, presumably of the Yam-els, one of over 20 bands that made up what historians refer to as the Kalapuyian division. According to her story, Chehalem was a local St. Patrick of sorts:

"At one time, so runs the legend, the Chehalem Valley was infested with rattlesnakes. They were everywhere, and very poisonous.

They would frequently bite the Indians and kill many of them. Chehalem told the snake king that he must stop this, but no attention being paid to these demands, Chehalem determined to stand it no longer. His people were dying too rapidly.

So he called together his medicine men and warriors. The warriors drove the snakes into their den, a rocky point said to have been on Sam Kinney's DLC. The medicine men then made medicine by which magic the old chief sealed up the mouth of the den.

For a whole moon he watched that none would escape. He neither ate nor slept during that time.

He was strong and vigorous when he began his vigil, but worn and wasted when he finished. The rattlers were his prisoners forever, and since then the valley has never seen one of them."

Lewis A. McArthur's standard reference guide, *Oregon Geographic Names,* tells a different story:

"It may be assumed that the modern word Chehalem comes from the Indian name Chahelim, listed under the heading Atfalati (Tualatin), Handbook of American Indians, *v. 1, p. 108. This name is given by Gatschet in 1877 to one of the bands of Atfalati, a division of the Kalapooian family of Indians. Gatschet lists more than 20 of these bands, all living in the general vicinity of the Chehalem Mountains. H.S. Lyman in the* Oregon Historical Quarterly, *v. 1, p. 323, refers to a point near the mouth of what is now known as Chehalem Creek and calls it* Cham-ho-kuc, *but gives no meaning or explanation."*

From early Newberg pioneer Joseph B. Rogers we get yet another version.

By 1847, Rogers was operating a ferry across the Willamette River just south of present-day downtown known to us today as Rogers Landing. Late in life, Joseph platted a town on his property he called "Chehalem."

It was his understanding he was using an Indian word meaning "Valley of the Flowers."

Finally, on a website the Oregon Wine Board had up in 2008, now gone, the definition of Chehalem was given as "gentle valley." ❖

Newberg and the Wheat Empire of the Willamette Valley

L ooking at 19th century maps of that stretch of the Willamette River north of Salem and south of Champoeg, three towns show up that time and changing conditions have erased from the face of the earth.

Sporting the names Fairfield, Wheatland and Lincoln, in their heyday they were points of departure for the wheat and livestock local farmers shipped to Portland and the world markets beyond. Their rise was meteoric, the fall a bit slower, each one eventually put out of business by soil exhaustion, the railroads that began crisscrossing the Willamette Valley in the 1870s, and the ability of other river towns to better diversify their economies.

These locations, all close neighbors to Newberg, live now mostly on the pages of old yellowed newspapers hidden away in county museums or in the memories of the descendants of long-gone residents, each a ghost-like reminder of what was once the Wheat Empire of the Willamette Valley.

So why did Newberg, also a river town, survive and these others vanish? The question has fascinated me for a long time and I'll attempt to answer it as we conclude this feature. First the background.

Even though the growing of wheat has never been confined to one particular part of the valley, the area most important to this story is that roughly bounded on the north by St. Paul and the south by Mission State Park, and on the east and west banks of the river by Highway 219 (River Road) and Highway 221 respectively.

Through this luscious farmland runs the mid-section of the Willamette River. From the 1850s up to about the 1880s, along a river turned wheat superhighway, one could find large clusters of grain storage facilities and cattle pens, the towns that built them, and scores of riverboats of various sizes servicing them.

Fairfield

We begin at Fairfield, located on the east side of our imaginary rectangle, 5.3 miles south of St. Paul in the vicinity of Marthaler Road.

As early as 1852, it was a considerable jumping off place for wheat, rivaling and eventually surpassing Champoeg as the principal shipping center closest to Portland. Fairfield grew simply because area farmers didn't have to travel as far to get to the boats. Also, the bluffs were higher, meaning the town escaped the destructive flood waters of 1861 that took out Champoeg and other low-lying river towns all the way to Corvallis and beyond.

Taking less than a decade, Fairfield could boast of a Presbyterian church, a post office, a school, three stores, a saloon and sawmill, a cooperage, a brickyard, numerous private dwellings and several large grain houses. Docks for the cargo boats stretched along the river banks.

By the early 1880s, Fairfield was past its zenith. In the 1940s, one could still see the church, a school, a saloon turned house and a decaying pile of squared timbers. Except for a cemetery a mile beyond Marthaler (not visible from the highway), nothing for certain survives from the town, although local tradition suggests a grain shed that may have been one of the town's stores currently sits on private property in the area. A mile south on the River Road, the Fairfield Grange, dating to 1929, is charming but not part of the original town.

Wheatland

Pioneer Daniel Matheny began the town of Wheatland in 1847 with a public sale of lots. Its location was on the west bank at mile marker 72, and a mile north of Jason Lee's Mission Bottom on the opposite shore. He had wanted to call the town Atchison, but it never stuck with the locals. In 1843 the site was the Beers and O'Neil ferry crossing, which was taken over by Matheny when he bought the O'Neil Provisional Land Claim in 1844. The boat that came with the sale was the first of the pioneer period with size enough to haul a wagon and ox team. Today, the Wheatland Ferry, the oldest and busiest ferry service in the state, still crosses at this point. The diesel-powered vessel in use is named the *Daniel Matheny V*.

The lots did sell, a warehouse was constructed, and a town quickly began to develop. With the arrival of the steamboats in the 1850s, Wheatland soon enjoyed shops, mills, saloons, a shingle-making plant, warehouses, two hotels, a school, churches and dwellings. The hotels, the Occidental and the Wheatland House, were said to have the best accommodations on the river between Oregon City and Salem. Boats landed daily, bringing freight and settlers upriver, later returning to Portland with livestock, grain and other farm produce for export.

By the 1880s, over 320 residents populated the area and the local flour mill was shipping 40,000 barrels of flour annually. Wheatland was large enough to have upper and lower sections until the 1861 flood took out the lower. Carried away were whole structures and thousands of bushels of wheat.

Lincoln

Originally known as Doak's Ferry after founder Andrew Jackson Doak, Lincoln on the west bank was the largest wheat port on the upper river. In a single year, shipments could run as high as 350,000 bushels, a record surpassed only by Portland. The east bank landing opposite the town was known as Spong's Ferry or Spong's Landing.

As wheat production on the west side surpassed that of French Prairie, the row of warehouses and wharves at Lincoln extended half a mile. It was not uncommon at these facilities to have a hundred farmers waiting in line to be served. Many had traveled from as far away as Willamina or Rickreal, often bypassing closer shipping points for the advantages afforded here.

The town was named for Abraham Lincoln by Jesse Walling of Salem in 1860. Even to the 1890s, when river commerce was but a shadow of its former self, Lincoln enjoyed six boats a day, three each way. Travel time from Portland was eight hours. The record was five and a half hours, put in by Miles Bell, captain of the steamer *Ruth*.

Lincoln's grist mill had grinding stones imported from Scotland and boasted a sawmill that could cut 5,000 board feet a day. Unlike Wheatland, with its fine hotels, Lincoln was never really a place of residence. If someone wanted to spend the night, it was usually on a bedroll in one of the warehouses.

With the building of the railroad through McCoy, only eight miles to the west, the town that Howard Corning so aptly described as the "Metropolis of Wheat" in his book *Willamette Landings*, began to dry up. By the late 1880s, as few as 50 residents populated the once-thriving area. Nothing survives of Lincoln except a sign on Highway 221 marking the approximate location.

So what about Newberg? Why them and not us?

Newberg was too far north to be of much service to wheat farmers in the central valley. Wheat was certainly grown here, however Yamhill County east never acquired the reputation for the crop enjoyed by other locations.

Evidence also suggests at least one wheat storage facility operated here, but Newberg's landing on the river never developed like its southern neighbors. There is no evidence to suggest there ever was that much interest on the part of the business community to do otherwise. Newberg's reluctance to use the other wheat landings as a business model helped save us. ❖

The ghost of North Main

A century ago, North Main was at the heart of what was Newberg's busiest commercial district. Not until just before World War I would it begin relinquishing its title to E. First, then die the slow death of a business location out of favor with local shoppers.

In its heyday, folks here would simply have known the thoroughfare as "Main Street." In an earlier life it had been the old pioneer wagon road connecting the Grubby End to West Chehalem and beyond to Carlton and Yamhill.

To illustrate how busy this street was, let's break it down block-by-block in roughly the distance from E. First (known then as "First Street") north past Ray's and Jem 100 to the railroad tracks.

The time frame we're dealing with would be the 1890s and early 1900s. The streets were platted 60 feet wide and the names used then are still around today.

Next to the tracks between Sherman and Sheridan on the west side was Christensen's (also spelled Christenson) Grain Elevator (later named Chehalem Valley Mills), with a storage facility on the south side of the tracks and a passenger and freight depot on the north side of the tracks directly across from the grain elevator. Next to the elevator to the south was a livery stable.

A drug store sat at the northwest corner of Sheridan and Main. A general merchandise store occupied the lot on the southwest corner. On the same block was a hardware store and a barbershop. Up and down the street were water wells, some with hoses permanently attached to be at the ready in case of fire.

Staying on the west side, from Hancock south to First, were two furniture stores and a stable. Later, a meat market and a dance hall made appearances. A doctor's office sat nearby.

Moving to the east side, for lovers of the "outlandish weed," a tobacco shop stood at the corner of Main and First in what today would be within the parking lot at Nap's. Later, it would become a print shop.

From First Street north to Hancock was yet another furniture store. Moving up the block to Sheridan was a store selling agricultural implements, next door an office, and next to that, Armory Hall, complete with a large stage used for plays, music, lectures and the like. Later, a storage shed for chairs and a photo shop arrived near this location.

From Sheridan north to Sherman was the Arlington Hotel. The location at some point became the M.H. Pinney Lumber Yard.

North Main would also enjoy a second hotel, the Commercial Hotel (later Hotel Purdy) at the southeast corner of Main and Sheridan.

Let's also note that Brey and Moores Fruit Drier Plant and the Oregon Handle Manufacturing Company would spring up just to the north near the railroad tracks.

So what's left from the old days? Not much. Chehalem Valley Mills survives and is a local treasure. North of the tracks on the west side sits the old Dunkard Brethren Church (now a private residence on the northwest corner of Franklin) and the original St. Peter's Catholic Church in the next block.

Because the photographic record of North Main is so thin, most of what I know about this historic street comes from the Newberg Public Library's collection of "Sanborn Maps," priceless gems of history compiled from 1867 through 1970 by the Sanborn-Perris Map and Publishing Company of New York City to help insurance companies assess property values for thousands of cities and towns across America.

A Wiki website outlining their history tells us "they are held in the paper and microfilm collections of historical societies, town halls, state archives and public and university libraries, and are of considerable value for their block-by-block portrayal of street patterns, lot lines and the placement, size, shape and use of buildings."

For the vast majority of locations for which they are available, the information they contain can be found nowhere else.

Items typically portrayed for Newberg (located in the Newberg Public Library) include cabins, private residences, warehouses, business establishments, churches, dance halls, bowling alleys, train depots, storage facilities, livery stables, hotels, grain elevators, the names of streets (and how wide), and much more.

Each Sanborn map represents a snapshot in time, and for Newberg, these snapshots came in 1891, 1892, 1905, 1912, and 1929. By comparing one set of maps to an earlier or later set, patterns of urban growth and decline are better facilitated. ❖

"Grubby End" no more

One hundred years ago, Newberg had the luxury of two weekly newspapers, *The Newberg Graphic* and *The Newberg Enterprise*.

On Oct. 11, 1912, *Enterprise* Editor and Proprietor John T. Bell published a one-time tabloid named the "Progress Edition."

For that generation, this special publication's stories, profiles, advertisements and photographs provided a measuring stick for how much Newberg had grown since its incorporation in 1889. For us today, it represents a nice snapshot of this city a century in our rear.

Bell also produced the "Progress Edition" to serve as a recruiting tool for the community.

Newberg wanted and needed new residents, businesses, farmers and families and the enterprising newspaperman went out of his way to let the world know the city and the nearby West Chehalem Valley had the credentials to be considered an Oregon "center of prosperity."

Though never stated, only implied, Bell's nifty tabloid also represented the end of the "Grubby End" spirituality that had prevailed during the 19th century. Newberg in 1912 was shedding its grubby image…a good place to raise a family but not necessarily the best place to be a farmer… to remake itself for the future.

I say this because I suspect no one at that time thought the "Grubby End" moniker would have the kind of sizzle and pop needed to recruit newcomers. Certainly not Mr. Bell.

Reading Bell today, here are some of the interesting aspects of life in Newberg he wanted folks to know:

City government consisted of a City Council (formerly known as "aldermen") and seven public officials referred to as the "Board of Officials": mayor, recorder, water superintendent, marshal, night marshal, street commissioner and engineer.

The publication devoted pages and pages to the agricultural bounty that was available in and around the city.

George Fox University was known as Pacific College. The student body was almost entirely Quaker.

Newberg's public schools enrolled 913 students, 183 in high school. Twenty-six teachers did the work. The youngest pupils attended classes in a wooden building known as the Graded School Building. It was located where the Chehalem Cultural Center is today.

A new high school had been built in 1910. It's still with us. Located at 714 Sixth Street and historically known as the Edwards School, the current use of the facility is to house the administrative offices of the Newberg Public School System.

An interesting school tidbit was contributed by City Superintendent A.C. Stanbrough, who wrote: "Several years ago Newberg adopted the centralization idea and a wagon is used to bring pupils from outlying parts of the district. This was the first district in the state to adopt such a course."

Does this mean Newberg was the first in Oregon to have "school busses?" It's tantalizing to think so.

Stanbrough also shared his pride in the fact that Newberg was listed on what he called the "accredited list of schools." This meant that if you graduated from Newberg High, you were automatically "admitted to the various colleges of the state without examination."

In 1912, the city had just brought online a new Carnegie library, thanks to the work of a civic-minded group known as the Ladies' Wednesday Club.

Indeed, the new library building was but one jewel in a number of other developments which spelled new levels of prosperity for the area.

Streets were being paved (including approaches to town from east and west), electricity was expanding, courtesy of the Yamhill Electric Company, and a new electric passenger train service was about to service Newberg under the auspices of the Portland, Eugene and Eastern Railway (PE&E) Company.

A second electric passenger train offering was also in the works, this by the Oregon Electric Railway Company (OERC), promising in a full page ad that "service would soon be introduced to Newberg and McMinnville."

Fearing competition by the OERC would hurt its presence in western Oregon, the Southern Pacific railway company bought PE&E in 1912. By 1914 this service was operating as the Red Electric passenger train line, connecting downtown Newberg to Portland and the rest of the Willamette Valley. OERC did provide trains to the valley but they went through the small town of Donald, 10 miles to the east.

The rose was the unofficial flower of the city and at the center of an annual Rose Festival hosted by the mayor and the business community. A feature of these annual fetes was a "procession of babies on the principal street (E. First) in their little carriages decorated with flowers."

The largest payrolls in town were provided by a logging company, a flour mill, a meat packing plant, a brick and tile works, a handle factory and a prune packing plant.

Was editor Bell's work all in vain? Was his "Progress Edition" a strong enough magnet to pull people to the "Grubby End?" Yes, at least in part. I also thought about this when I read the following:

"It does not require a very keen intelligence," Bell stated, "to see the future is bright. Before many years, all the hills around Newberg will be dotted with fine residences and highly improved small tracts."

Well said, good fellow. ❖

The great Newberg bank robbery

This is the story of what may be the greatest bank robbery attempt in Newberg history.

It happened on Oct. 19, 1903, and it's worth retelling on a number of levels.

As the details unfold, you quickly realize this would make a great scene in a movie. These are usually the best kinds of stories.

It happened at a time when banks still carried gold. In this case, the gold on deposit at the scene of the attempted robbery was owned by the people of the town.

The *Newberg Graphic* interviewed a number of eyewitnesses to file its report for the Oct. 23 issue, but no one with a badge. Apparently, Newberg didn't have a police force at that time. The area had a marshal, Joe Woods, but he was nowhere to be found. It was up to the citizens of the town to respond to the threat. And respond they did, with an ingenuity that inspires lovers of local history all these many years later.

But enough of the teasers.

The robbery began on a foggy Monday night. At 30 minutes past three in the morning, the fire bell began ringing, which was what Newberg did back then when there was an emergency.

As folks rushed into the streets, they looked for a fire. Seeing and smelling none, attention began to concentrate on the east side of Center Street, between First and Second. This was the location of the Bank of Newberg. Talk began rocketing through the crowd that an attempted robbery had just happened, with undetermined results.

They were correct. What they didn't know but would find out over the next several days was that the robbers had actually entered the bank at midnight. The burglars next began the job of tearing a hole through a wall that would put them inside the bank vault.

Above where they were working was an apartment rented by a woman and her two brothers from the state of Washington. They were of the Maxfield family.

It didn't take long for the woman and one of her brothers to be awakened by the loud, banging noises coming from downstairs. Looking out the window, they saw two strange men on the street standing guard. Both were carrying rifles.

At 2:30 p.m., an explosion shook the building. It cut through the nearby neighborhood like a bolt of lightening. The Maxfields told the *Graphic*, "It seemed at times like the building would be shaken down."

Then, another explosion, and another. The bombardment went on for 30 minutes. The robbers appeared unconcerned they might be caught.

The second Maxfield brother remained asleep. The newspaper commented: "It is evident Gabriel will have to give an extra toot for his benefit for the day that's coming."

Down the street, one of those aroused was the principal of the high school, R.W. Kirk. He remembered nine separate explosions. To him and others, the repeated attempts represented the "desperate nerve of the artists in charge."

Isaac Vinson had been out late and was walking toward the bank when the cacophony began. He heard one of the armed guards yell, "Get out of this you (expletive deleted) or I'll put a hole through you."

To back up the command, the lookout sent a rifle shot in Vinson's direction.

At the same time, Seaman W. Potter, a jeweler, optician and minister, grabbed his handgun and headed for the front door. His wife reached for his coat and pulled him back just as the bullet shot at Vinson whined down the street. He figured the warning given by the guard's rifle meant him as well, so he didn't try and press the issue.

Credit for warning the town settled on Arthur Austin, son of Henry Austin, A-dec co-founder Ken Austin's grandfather.

Sizing up the situation, Arthur ran for the fire bell tower near the center of town. Arriving there, he looked for the pull rope to ring the bell. It was gone, taken by the robbers before they had made their way down the street to the bank.

Climbing up through the darkness to the top of the tower, the young man pushed on the bell with his hands. The ring was loud and clear. To reinforce the point, he began shooting in the air with a pistol.

The town came running. The robbers fled the scene and headed north toward Portland.

Later, investigators indicated nitroglycerin had been used in the attempted robbery, most of which was leveled at a strong box inside the vault. Unflinching, the heavily damaged box refused to give up its precious contents.

Reported the *Graphic*:

"When the door was finally forced open (by bank officials) and the sacks of gold coin found undisturbed, cashier John C. Colcord gave vent to his feelings in one wild hoop." ❖

The night the lights came on

In this story we celebrate the Newberg Fire Department's tradition of decorating our city with lights, scrolls and wreaths each holiday season.

Let's begin by going back to when the tradition started.

The date was Tuesday, Christmas Eve, 1929.

Prior to '29, the concept of a Christmas symbol belonging to everyone was not a part of the Grubby End culture.

Celebrations involving more than the individual family were typically church affairs. Denominations marked the holly jolly season with religious services, choir and orchestra concerts, special Yuletide lectures, door-to-door caroling, eats, treats and everything in-between.

In the meantime, the practice of decorating a large tree, then putting it in the middle of a downtown street to arouse the community's Christmas spirit had become trendy in other Oregon locations.

Not to be outdone, during the late fall of '29, the local fire boys decided Newberg should do the same, but deferred taking action on the activity.

Their hope was that some other local organization would like the idea and get it done.

It wasn't that the guys were lazy. In addition to fighting fires and providing other rescue-type services for the city, the firemen were busy sponsoring a three-act play titled, "Headstrong Joan." Recruiting the players, holding rehearsals and selling tickets left little time for anything extra.

Now if this sounds a little bit out of character for a fire department, remember, the decade of the 1920s was the golden age of community theater in small town America, with everyone (pardon the pun) getting in on the act.

Often, the productions were fundraisers. They were always good-will raisers.

The latter was certainly true of Newberg Fire, as it was always looking for ways to present a good image of itself to townsfolk who, more often than not, considered recruits, in the words of a *Graphic* reporter, "a rough and ready bunch, too often criticized rather than praised."

At some point, this whole Christmas tree idea became a textbook example of the old axiom, "If it's everybody's responsibility, it's nobody's responsibility."

As Christmas week approached, not one group had stepped forward to help out.

To remedy the situation, the fire department quickly assembled a committee, secured a big tree in the local woods and named it the "Community Tree." It was hauled to downtown on Christmas Eve and put in the middle of the street at the intersection of Howard and First, right in front of City Hall.

With financial assistance from the Chamber of Commerce, 1,000 bags stuffed with candy, nuts and oranges were assembled for the kids.

When the tree lights finally came on, blinking and twinkling their Christmas magic to the crowd, the Claude Cummings Orchestra played "Holy Night" and the party was on.

After greetings by Pacific College President Levi Pennington, the Junior Leaguers of the Methodist Episcopal Church contributed more carols.

And then...finally... the big man with the red suit and "ho ho ho" made his entrance.

The kids squealed with delight.

Friends and relatives of George Candeaux, the man behind the white beard, gave a knowing smile.

The firemen shook hands and patted each another on the back.

And all was right with the world.

The *Graphic* reported later: "The firemen are giving notice they will hold a community Christmas tree and program again next year and with an early start they anticipate an even more successful event."

Indeed! ❖

Hats off to Highway 99W

In the old days, highways were not so much about speed as they were about promoting commerce.

That Route 66 went straight through the hearts of hundreds of towns on its way across America was no accident. It quickly earned its moniker, "The Main Street of America."

Here on the West Coast, we had our own version of Route 66. It was Highway 99W, Newberg's "main street" since 1919.

Today it runs through historic downtown via two one-way streets. Eastbound travelers use E. First; Hancock handles the westbound.

At the "splits," which bookend our city center, the highway becomes two-way once again. The east split is at the big flag pole across from Hoover Park. On the west side, it's at the Dairy Queen.

For decades, traffic downtown along E. First was two-way. The flow changed in 1976.

From 1919-1930, that is, from the road's first construction until it was incorporated into the national highway system as a piece of U.S. Route 99W, it was known as Oregon Highway 3 or the Capitol Highway. Travelers used this road as the major route between Salem and Portland on the west side of the Willamette River.

Highway 3 was also the first paved highway built by the newly formed (at that time) State Highway Commission, under the direction of legendary bridge builder C.B. McCullough.

A former engineering professor at Oregon State University, McCullough later supervised the construction of over 700 bridges in the state, including all the major spans on the Oregon Coast.

The last section of the famous road to be paved and opened to traffic in this part of the county was the stretch between Chehalem Creek and McMinnville. The year was 1935. The project provided much needed jobs during the Great Depression.

From 1926 to 1964, U.S. Route 99 was the principal transportation route on the West Coast from Calexico, Calif., on the U.S.-Mexico border to Blaine, Wash., on the U.S.-Canada border.

It divided at Junction City north of Eugene to travel both sides of the Willamette River to Portland. Thus, there was also a U.S. Route 99E through towns such as Salem, Woodburn, Aurora and Oregon City.

Like so many early highways, U.S. Route 99 followed old horse and stagecoach trails. Other names it answered to included the Pacific Highway, The Golden Chain Route and the Highway of Three Nations. In California it was known as the Golden State Highway.

The original route in Yamhill and surrounding counties west of the river was Salem to Dayton on Highway 221, then Dayton to Portland through Dundee and

Newberg on Highway 3. At some point, the Dayton/Salem section was bypassed in favor of the route still in use, that is, McMinnville, Amity and Rickreall to Corvallis, Monroe and Junction City.

Among the hundreds of roadside businesses given birth by U.S. Route 99W, A&W Root Beer first opened in Lodi, Calif., in 1919.

Of the 30 or so drive-in movie theaters that once dotted the highway across three states, only Newberg's 99W Drive-In remains. A second theater, the Puget Park Drive-in in Everett, Wash., closed in January 2010.

Like all major U.S. highways built during the 1920s and '30s, U.S. 99 incorporated short and long stretches of pre-existing roads. Around Newberg and vicinity, this was the Capitol Highway.

In 1930, Highway 3 was renamed U.S. Route 99W and then in 1972 it became Oregon 99W. Today, 99W east of Hess Creek is known as the Portland Road. At Providence Newberg Hospital it becomes 99W or the Herbert Hoover Highway. Through the Rex Hill neighborhood, older residents sometimes refer to this stretch as the Pacific Highway.

If all this seems confusing, it is.

For those who like to travel the bypassed routes of old highways, here are several nearby options:

Between Newberg and Sherwood, there are two small pieces of the old road. Head up Rex Hill, go past Haugen Road and look to the left for Garland Road. Here you will see a sign that says "SW Old Pacific Highway West." Closer to Sherwood, turn right at the Timberline Baptist Church on SW Brookman Road, go one block and look for the "SW Old Highway 99" sign at the intersection.

On the west side of Newberg, past the Dairy Queen and just before the Shell station, turn on to 2nd Way Street, then left and left again on a remnant marked "Old 99." Follow the road into a mobile home park to a dead end at Chehalem Creek, presumably where an earlier bridge crossing used to be.

Between Dundee and Lafayette at the Highway 18 intersection, be sure to visit McDougal Road, probably the best-preserved piece of old 99W in this part of the county.

For a flavor of the original route from west into McMinnville, turn left on Lafayette Street, right on 5th Street, an immediate left to Irvine and then a right on to 3rd and through the heart of downtown.

Ready for a real adventure?

The author's favorite stretch of old 99W is down in Polk County, south out of Monmouth, through rolling farmland toward the 1928 bridge at the Luckiamute River and Helmick State Park, Oregon's first state park. From the main route of 99, the old road sits across open fields just to the west.

This is the perfect place to experience what your grandparents knew when they took to the open road: half the destination was the view out the window. ❖

Celebrating women's suffrage

The year 1912 was a year of triumph and tragedy.
It was the year of the sinking of the *Titanic*, the year of the founding of the Boy and Girl Scouts, the year Harriet Quimby became the first woman to fly over the English Channel, only to die two months later in a plane crash.

Future First Lady Pat Nixon, singers Woody Guthrie and Perry Como, and comedians Art Linkletter and Minnie Pearl were born. The fictional "Tarzan" first appeared in a pulp magazine. Nurse Clara Barton died. So did Dracula's Bram Stoker.

It was an Olympic year, with the games held in Stockholm, Sweden. In 1912, we elected a new president, Democrat Woodrow Wilson, in a 435 Electoral College landslide victory.

Here in Oregon, 1912 was the year our state passed legislation legalizing women's suffrage, meaning the right for women to vote in statewide elections. The final count was 61,265 for and 57,104 against. Only men cast ballots. After five earlier tries—1884, 1900, 1906, 1908 and 1910—the guys had finally gotten it right.

The following is also fact: No other state in the nation took six times to give women political equality in the voting booth. In the West, we were also one of the last states to do so, with Wyoming, Utah, Colorado, Idaho and Washington out in the lead, Alaska and Nevada bringing up the rear. California also said yes to suffrage in 1912.

The best "pictures" we have of Newberg 100 years ago are to be found among the pages of the two newspapers that were around at the time, both published once a week. They were the *Newberg Enterprise* (a Friday paper) and the *Newberg Graphic* (Thursday).

The election was held on Tuesday, Nov. 5. The ballot that day, I kid you not, was nine feet long. We can only imagine the time it took for each person to vote. Oregon's "initiative and referendum system" was alive and well. In addition to an amendment to allow statewide suffrage, there were 37 other acts, extensions, separations, exemptions, laws and revisions for voters to consider.

One would abolish the death penalty, another would give the state approval to operate its own printing plant, and still another would replace all taxes with a single tax. Twenty-four were defeated, 14 passed (none of the ones I've mentioned made it through).

But we're here to celebrate the positive result for women's suffrage, which begs the question, what was the reaction here locally?

I went into the research for this column with big expectations for coverage…and plenty of blank paper for notes.

*Etienne Lucier in 1843.
(From a painting by
Theodore Gegoux)*

*As much as the covered wagon, the Montreal Canoe helped conquer
the West. (Public Domain)*

*One of the earliest photos of Newberg when it was
known as the "Grubby End." (George Fox University
Archives)*

*William Hobson, shown here in the 1880s, did more to
establish the Society of Friends in Newberg and Yamhill
County than any other early settler.
(George Fox University Archives)*

The town the doughboys of World War I left behind. (George Fox University Archives)

Ewing Young lived in a cabin not far from what later became the location for the school west of Newberg that carried his name. (George Fox University Archives)

What the Old Fashioned Festival parade looked like in 1910. (George Fox University Archives)

Downtown Newberg after wood-framed buildings were replaced with brick buildings. The tracks were for the Red Electric trains that serviced Newberg from c. 1913 through the late 1920s. (George Fox University Archives)

When N. Main was in its prime, c. early 1900s. (Photo courtesy Kathleen Watson)

The home of Graphic *editor and publisher E.H. Woodward. The house still stands on N. River Street, a stone's throw south of GFU. (George Fox Archives)*

Will and Jessie Purdy in the early 1900s. Will owned the Purdy Hotel on N. Main and later entered politics at the state level. (Photo courtesy Kathleen Watson)

Newberg's Public Library after its construction in 1912 with funds from the Carnegie Foundation. (George Fox University Archives)

The Spaulding Paper Mill was a major employer for early Newberg. (George Fox University Archives)

Early home of the Newberg Graphic *and the Bank of Newberg, 817 E. 1st. (George Fox University Archives)*

Cover Photo: *Morris and Miles Dry Goods, c. 1890s. Probably the oldest surviving business structure in Newberg. Still in business in 2014 as Chapter's Bookstore. (George Fox University Archives)*

Wood-Mar Hall in 1911, still the crown jewel of the GFU campus. (George Fox University Archives)

Scott Leavitt as he looked in his official U.S. House of Representatives photo, c. 1930. (Public Domain)

Billy Sullivan festival pin from the town where he attended high school. (Public Domain)

Maybelle Jette's official KKK mug, 1923. (Photo courtesy Steven Kenney)

Goat Woman on George Fox campus, 1957. (Photo courtesy John Lyda)

Burt Brown Barker (wearing hat) and former president Herbert Hoover, the day of the dedication of Hoover Park, Aug. 10, 1955. (George Fox University Archives)

President Hoover and retired GFU President Levi Pennington, August 1955. (George Fox University Press)

Hoover-Minthorn House Museum, Newberg's oldest surviving house and boyhood home of Herbert Hoover. (George Fox University Archives)

The Cameo Theater, landmark of the downtown Newberg business district, c. January 1939. (George Fox University Archives)

The 1933 Oregon State Agricultural College "Iron Immortals." NUH Football Coach Vernon Wedin is in the second row, far left. (Photo courtesy the OSU Alumni Association)

A rare photo of the extraordinary Jennie Miller, who is standing with a cane on the front row. (Photo from writer's personal collection)

Ruth Stoller, one of the most gifted Yamhill County historians of all time. (Photo courtesy Marjorie Owens and the Yamhill County Historical Society).

T-2 Tanker similar to SS Newberg. *(Public Domain)*

Jesse Edwards House, built 1883. (Council of Independent Colleges)

O.C. Yocum's Government Camp Hotel, 1927. (Photo by Everett Sickler)

Flooding on E. 1st Street, 1934. (Photo by Norman P. Riley)

On Thursday, Nov. 7, two days removed from the election, the *Graphic* had almost nothing. I thought…maybe too soon to make it to press…so I moved on to the *Enterprise* and its Nov. 8 edition.

Bingo, far left corner of the first page, one sentence reference that it passed, nothing else.

With eyebrows lifted in mild surprise, I looked at the rest of the front page and saw almost two columns from one Henry McGuire about the lack of a market for apples. He told the paper he was being forced to use the current crop as hog feed, about 200 bushels worth.

I kept looking. Surely, this was a bigger story than a bunch of hungry hogs.

I found more.

I saw another small section showing suffrage had carried by 113 votes. Also, 308 had cast ballots against the state engaging in the printing business, 85 more voters than those wanting to abolish capital punishment, and that Wilson had received 46 more tallies than presidential incumbent William Howard Taft.

What's going on here? Why the lack of attention?

The following day, I came back for another round of spelunking. I stuck it rich in the *Graphic*. What I found I had never considered.

Said Publisher and Editor E.H. Woodward on Nov. 21, 1912:

"The Oregonian is twenty years behind the times. The city of Dayton held an election Monday (Nov. 18) and the women voted. The following morning, the Oregonian said: 'Mrs. Ella Harris of Dayton has cause of pride for she is the first Oregon woman to vote.' Women have been voting at the annual city elections in Newberg ever since the city was incorporated (1889), more than twenty years ago. The little matter of women voting is such a common feature of the city elections in Newberg that it makes a Newberger smile to read the big spiel from Dayton…"

On Nov. 30, 1912, in the presence of Oregon Governor Oswald West and Dr. Viola M. Coe, important state leader in the equal rights movement, suffragist Abigail Scott Duniway signed the bill (Section 2, Article 11 of the state constitution) she had drafted earlier, legalizing a woman's right to vote in the state of Oregon. It was s landmark day for the Beaver state and one I hope we are still celebrating a thousand years from now.

It would not be until after World War I that Oregon's women voters could cast ballots at the national level, made possible by Congress in 1919 through passage of the 19th amendment to the U.S. Constitution. ❖

Newberg during the Great Depression

What were Newberg and Yamhill County like during the 1930s, the decade of The Great Depression? Get ready for some surprises. So much of it simply doesn't fit the stereotypical model we have carried forward from then to the present.

(Note: Please know the author recognizes there were many Newberg families who had to sacrifice a lot in the 1930s just to make ends meet. It is not the intent of this story for these remarks to diminish the hard times the reader's relatives may have gone through during this trying period in our nation's history.)

In 1930, the Yamhill Electric Company spent $100,000 on improvements. In 1931, the company showed a net profit of $70,000 and was also a major PGE stockholder.

That same year, the West Coast Telephone Company announced $24,000 in improvements to the city's telephone system.

Gas service was first made available to Newberg in 1931 by Portland Gas and Coke. Gains in the number of customers using gas, in their usage of gas, and in their purchases of gas equipment increased every year during the 1930s. From 1935 to 1938, gas business grew 84 percent.

By the end of the 1930s, Newberg could boast of 20 churches.

There were the same number of service stations and garages.

In 1935, Pacific Highway (99W) from Chehalem Creek to McMinnville was opened.

In 1936, Newberg welcomed the addition of a new brick post office on East First. It's the one we use today.

In 1935, if you watered your lawn there was a "sprinkling charge" of $1 per 5,000 gallons. In 2012 dollars, this was approximately $17.

On July 25, 1935, *The Newberg Graphic* reported 50 new subscribers in one week, 27 renewals. By Sept. 1, the *Graphic* had added 141 new subscribers, mixed with 119 renewals.

In July, Claude Pearson, his wife, and Walt Nichols drove to Detroit, Mich., to pick up new Hudson and Terraplane autos. The three cars they drove east each pushed a new car on the way back. They left Newberg on Wednesday and arrived in Detroit on Sunday. The return trip took seven days.

On Feb. 5, 1936, over 500 attended a banquet to charter a Rotary Club for Newberg.

By 1938, Newberg enjoyed 12 restaurants.

In 1935, planning began to build a new high school, Newberg Union High. It opened in the fall of 1939 at a cost of $250,000; $132,000 of that was federal. The one million board feet of lumber used in the building was supplied by the L.H.L. Company of Carlton. The auditorium was equipped with 816 seats.

In 1934, Pacific College set an enrollment record. It was broken one year later.

In 1935, the library was in an expansive mood and bought new books.

On March 19, 1936, all teachers in Newberg were rehired for the fall with an 8.2 percent pay increase.

From 1930-35, the county enjoyed an increase of 245 new farms.

In the 1930s, Yamhill County became Oregon's third largest producer of turkeys, behind Linn and Douglas counties.

We led the state in walnut production, with 6,000 acres planted. Filbert production went from 5 percent of the nation's output to 50 percent. The demand for filberts far exceeded supply. Approximately 650 growers were involved and processing facilities everywhere were installing new equipment and hiring new workers.

Yamhill County ranked eighth in the U.S. for the production of prunes.

We had 20,000 acres devoted to peaches, pears and cherries.

Throughout the Depression, dairy farming was the chief agricultural pursuit in the Willamette Valley, as the number of milk cows increased from 88,336 in 1930 to 118,350 in 1939. In Yamhill County milk cows increased from 8,128 to 11,350 during the same time period.

The county operated 13 farmer's co-ops.

In 1938, the Dundee Nut Growers Association processed and packed 1,300 TONS of walnuts, the largest crop ever.

A popular musical group was Sue's Kitchen Band, in which 14 ladies who were members of the local Home Economics Club played instruments made of items found around the kitchen. ❖

A history of newspapers in Newberg

The city's first newspaper was not *The Newberg Graphic* but the *Newberg Banner.*
It was sponsored by the Newberg Debating Society, with the first issue appearing Nov. 23, 1878. William Noah Parrish was the editor.

The NDS was formed in December 1877 by prominent pioneer families in the small community of East Chehalem, which today (roughly) would be everything starting at Hess Creek and going east to where Portland Road becomes 99W and lifts up to Rex Hill.

Historian Doris Huffman states in her delightful study of the Everest family (10 members participated) that the group's roster numbered 60, dues were 25 cents (charged to the men only), and meetings were held on Saturday nights at the Brutscher schoolhouse, located today out in the vicinity of Fred Meyer and the Providence Newberg Hospital.

Huffman said the purpose of the NDS was to "promote intellectual, social and moral advancement, and familiarization with Parliamentary usage."

The Banner also served another purpose. It boosted membership in the society. Contents of the paper would be discussed at meetings. Folks who couldn't read would show up just to hear what was going on.

One dollar was levied against any member who wrote something insulting about another; it was 50 cents additional if it made the paper.

Huffman added that among the society's favorable deliberations "women have more influence over men than money; a dog is of more benefit to a man than a gun."

The Banner continued until 1885, when it ceased for reasons still not exactly clear.

Undaunted, the society launched another newspaper, the *Evening Star.* It was handwritten and edited by local teacher and Newbergian of many talents, Joseph S. Everest.

It disappeared in 1889. According to the 1989 publication, *Century to Remember,* the reason was, "it couldn't compete with the *Graphic,* which was produced on a printing press."

The *Newberg Graphic's* first issue rolled off the press on Dec. 1, 1888. On Feb. 21, 1889, the town of Newberg was incorporated. So the *Graphic* is 83 days older than the city that has been its home for 125 years and holds the distinction of being Newberg's oldest business.

The Graphic was started by a Californian named John C. Hiatt of Whittier, Calif., publisher for many years of the *Whittier Graphic.*

Hiatt never moved to Newberg. Instead, he gave the paper to his son, Will. In thinking about his future, it didn't take long for the young man to realize journalism was a bad fit.

The elder Hiatt immediately put the paper up for sale. Local resident Samuel Hobson bought it and turned it over to his son, Frank, and a family friend named O.V. Allen.

By December 1889 the *Graphic* would change hands again and again until ownership finally stabilized under the direction of Quaker E. H. Woodward, who kept the paper until 1921. This 30-year period was the *Graphic's* "golden age," when its influence over local public opinion was at its greatest.

In 1894, *The Yamhill Independent* emerged in the community with Newberg Mayor Orm C. Emery as editor. It was owned by the Newberg Printing Company.

Unlike the *Graphic*, which ran national news on the front page and local news inside, the *Independent* offered just the opposite. A one-year subscription cost $1.50. Like the *Banner*, there is no record of when it ceased to print.

Local publisher G.A. Graves introduced his *Newberg Enterprise* in February 1901. The paper stayed in business until June 13, 1918, when a fire destroyed its First Street office. In the final edition, Graves thanked the *Graphic* for use of its printing press to produce his paper.

The *Newberg Scribe*, a Thursday weekly, began publishing in late 1931, under the direction of Editor John D. Burt, formerly of the *Carleton Sentinel*. He was later joined by Associate Editor Don Woodman, formerly of the *Yamhill Spokesman*.

In fact, when the *Scribe* was first introduced, it used *Newberg Scribe and Carleton Sentinel* as its official name. On Sept. 3, 1936, the *Scribe* was under the direction of new owners Bob Harper and Dick Dent.

In 1939, Harper sold his interest in the paper to Dent. On April 4, 1940, Dent helped merge the *Scribe* with the *Graphic*.

Thus, the *Scribe* became little more than a memory, except for the name, which appeared for several years during World War II on the *Newberg Graphic* masthead.

After the war, the *Chehalem Valley Times* appeared, owned and edited by George Graves and housed in a building on the southeast corner of First and Main streets.

In more recent times, Newberg has enjoyed the *Chehalem Valley News,* 1949-1952; the *Newberg Times*, 1983-1984; and the *Chehalem News*, 1995. In the late 1960s, the *Newberg News* was published for a brief period. In the 1980s, the *Newberg Weekly* made an appearance. ❖

Gone with the wind

It's often said that animals have a special sense about them, instincts that let them know something bad is about to happen.

On Friday, Oct. 12, 1962, this instinct was on full display at a nearby turkey farm.

At about 4:45 p.m., an entire flock of the big birds suddenly ran to the middle of the yard and bunched together as one big mass of gobble gobble.

The turkey grower tried to move them. They wouldn't budge.

In nearby Newberg, using slightly different instincts, folks looked forward to the weekend as they went about their usual Friday afternoon business.

At the high school, it was homecoming. Loran-Douglas Field would soon be rocking to the cheers of the Tiger faithful against the visitors from St. Helens.

At 4:55 p.m., the world suddenly changed. A wind storm slammed against Oregon so violent it left the state in shattered rubble for months.

Without the Weather Channel, modern Doppler radar, or 24-hour "smart" phone access to local climate conditions, modern conveniences still decades in the future, nearly everyone was caught by surprise. And the few who had heard something about a storm brewing were stunned by its intensity.

Popularly known as the Columbus Day Storm or the Big Blow, but officially referred to by weather historians as Typhoon Frieda (also spelled Freda), this extra-tropical cyclone traveling north from California hit the towns of western Oregon and beyond with winds that reached upwards of 140 mph.

An Air Force wind gauge atop Mt. Hebo (elev. 3,154 ft.) on the northern Oregon coast measured 160 mph before it blew apart.

Across Yamhill County, wind gusts exceeded 100 mph.

When Frieda was done, Newberg and the surrounding countryside looked like a war zone. There were downed trees and power lines, damaged barns, buildings, homes, road and yard debris, and animals on-the-loose for miles in all directions.

Across the Far West, the destruction was beyond comprehension. Nothing like it had been seen since the1906 San Francisco earthquake and fire.

In Oregon alone, over 64,000 homes, 5,000 businesses and 20 industrial plants experienced partial or severe damage, with combined losses totaling $170,000,000. In today's dollars, the amount would be over $4.2 billion.

Here are some more short sketches of the aftermath in Newberg, as reported in the *Graphic* on Thursday, Oct. 18, 1962.

-There was no loss of life in Newberg, although several injured had to be treated at Newberg Community Hospital. Across the region, from California to British Columbia, 46 people died.

-The roof of the Friendsview Manor carport collapsed, crushing Herbert Bryant's new Cadillac to a height of three feet!

-Hardest hit were the farmers. The District 29 school board released 750 students over a week-long period to help harvest the filbert and walnut crops at 30 orchards.

-Irene Jackson and her husband, Chuck, lost their home to a fallen tree. They rebuilt in the same location, on Coral Creek Road, where they have now lived for almost 60 years. "We stayed in our basement for nine years while our new home was being constructed," Irene said.

-Russell Gainer lost part of his house to a tree, but a solid glass greenhouse nearby went untouched. He was hunting in Wyoming at the time.

-Cameo Theater owner Ted Francis put a "Gone With The Wind' sign in front of his 99W Drive-In on Portland Road because the storm took out his giant screen and the sheet metal fence surrounding the property.

-A gal soaking in her tub when the storm hit got up, dried off, put on her bathrobe and went outside to see about the cause of the noise and commotion. According to the *Graphic*, "winds blew her bathrobe off her body and across the tops of nearby trees."

-Tom Roshak, 12 years old at the time, was at Buckley's Locker with his grandfather when transformers starting popping in the howling wind. "When we returned home to Coral Creek Road," he said, "we had lost over 110 prune trees."

-Friendsview residents Verne Martin and wife Ellen remember that Sherwood High was playing a "Catholic school" at home the night of the storm. The game, of course, was cancelled. When it was realized the visitors would not be able to get home, Verne remembers, "a call went out to the ladies of the community to help make tuna fish sandwiches because, as Catholics, they could not eat meat on Fridays."

-Newberg's homecoming game was postponed until Monday, Oct. 15. It was an afternoon contest, with few in attendance. The eastside bleachers had been torn down by the storm but the grandstand remained in good shape. The Tigers lost.

-Just before the storm, Mrs. O.V. Hubbel and her two children, Barry and Sharon, left by train for the Seattle World's Fair. The three Newberg residents sat in a passenger car with no food or water for the next 18 hours, waiting for crews to go ahead of the train and clear the tracks of fallen debris.

-*The Graphic* reported the local cleanup with these words: "It was a neighborly, community effort, reminiscent of pioneer days of 'barn raisings,' when everyone chipped in to help each other."

-Frieda tried its best to dislodge the turkeys from their spot in the yard. The turkeys won. ❖

History of Newberg Public Library

Newberg was the first city in Yamhill County to open a public library and the third to open one in the Portland metro area after Portland itself and Forest Grove. The date for us was 1907.

The Newberg Public Library, however, has antecedents that go back to 1858, when a local Sunday school class, with a possible affiliation to the Congregational Church in Portland, operated a small library for its students. The collection contained 160 volumes, mostly of the song-book variety, including the popular (at the time) *Sabbath School Gems.*

In the 1880s, the Newberg chapter of the Women's Temperance League (WTL) saw the need for a library and began buying books with money raised through subscriptions and sponsored entertainment.

One hundred sixty books were placed in the hands of J.T. Smith, an 1876 Iowa transplant, who operated a combination library, butcher shop, hardware store, drug store and post office all under one roof. In an article in the *Graphic* in February 1925, resident Jessie Britt recalled that borrowing from Smith cost 5 cents per book.

In the meantime, on March 19, 1891, the Whittier Literary Society, another early precursor, was organized by a group of the town's leading businessmen. It was created for the "mutual improvement of its members in all exercises of a literary character." They raised money through ticket sales and membership dues and used the funds to buy books, papers, magazines and other reading materials to circulate among its members.

In 1893, the books from Smith's store were turned over to Pacific College by the WTL. Smith moved north to Washington state to continue his career as an agent for the Pacific Coast Installment Library Association. As such, it is assumed that between the years 1893 and 1907 Newberg had no "library" to serve the general community.

On Nov. 10, 1907, 18 representatives from local civic organizations met in the dental office of a "Dr. Harold" to fill this void and discuss a public library for the city.

The group, soon to become the Newberg Library Association, was inspired by a decision of the Wednesday Club, a women's civic improvement organization, to provide financial support to the association though dues and fundraisers.

One week later the association held its first official meeting, where it was decided the library would be free. The City of Newberg Council entered into an agreement with the Newberg Library Association to levy a tax to support the library if the association would operate it. It was agreed and the library opened in a corner of the YMCA room in the building that had once been the Bank of Newberg on the northwest corner of First Street and Meridian, 817 E. First. The building can still be seen today.

The date for the opening was May 26, 1908. The first loan of a book was made on that date by the town's first librarian, Margaret Inglis.

Always tight for space at the YMCA, the collection was moved several times before association members realized something else had to be done. In other words, the collection needed a home.

In 1910, the association petitioned Andrew Carnegie himself for help. In one of the greatest philanthropic acts in American history, Carnegie at this time was giving away millions of dollars from his fortune to help towns across the country build libraries.

Knowing this, Newberg appointed a special library committee to begin working to attract Carnegie dollars to the "Grubby End" and soon received word from James Bertram, Mr. Carnegie's personal secretary, that $10,000 was on the way for bricks and mortar, provided Newberg could guarantee support of $1,000 a year to sustain the facility *and* provide a good site on which to build it.

The answer for both requirements was yes.

By 1911 Carnegie had approved the building plans and construction began in October. On March 29, 1912, the Newberg Carnegie Library was dedicated.

Lining the shelves of the 4,000-square-foot facility were 1,000 volumes, under the watchful eye of Ms. Inglis. With everything off to a new start, the association renamed itself the Newberg Carnegie Library Association.

The 1970s saw the formation of a regional library system allowing Newberg patrons to borrow books, now totaling more than a million volumes, from libraries in a multi-county area. Toward the end of the decade, crowded conditions in the original building necessitated the move toward expansion, which got under way in 1982.

In 1985, using a generous donation of land by A-dec co-owners Ken and Joan Austin, a private gift by the Publisher's Paper Company, Federal funding under the auspices of the Library Services and Construction Act, and voter-approval of $965,000 in construction bonds, expansion of the library moved forward. By 1986, Newberg had an additional 17,700-square feet in which to house books.

The 100th anniversary of the Newberg Library Association (and the so-called "YMCA library" on Meridian) was celebrated the week of May 26-31, 2008, with daily events that included a nonstop read-aloud by community members, live music, a Century Walkathon fundraiser, movies and refreshments.

March 29-31, 2012, the library noted Mr. Carnegie's gift with a centennial celebration that included an open house, lectures, and a trolley tour of historic downtown Newberg.

In the 100 years since the library was dedicated, the collection has grown from a thousand to over 90,000 books, audio and video materials, as well as online and other materials. Now that's something worth celebrating! ❖

History of the Old Fashioned Festival

Afavorite summer activity in Newberg is the Old Fashioned Festival. Currently, it runs four days at the end of July. Some folks who have lived here a long time still refer to it by a name we haven't used for 30 years: Old Fashioned Days.

A popular belief is that the Old Fashioned Festival began as the Newberg Berry Festival. This festival was inaugurated on July 9, 1921, by the city's most active and prestigious (at that time) civic organization, the Newberg Berrians.

In reality, the Berry Festival (later renamed the Berrian Festival) was inspired by and loosely patterned after five earlier summer celebrations held during the 1890s and up to around 1920. (Note: Pioneer Oregon loved community gatherings and so there may have been earlier ones than mentioned here.)

The first was something referred to in early issues of the Pacific College *Crescent* student publication which was called the Newberg Fair. No recollections of the event in print have come down to us so the name is all we know.

Next was a city-wide event held on July 4 known simply as "Independence Day." The third was called the Rose Show. The fourth marked a return to Independence Day under a new name, the Fourth of July Celebration.

Beginning in 1913, the celebration seems to have been held in conjunction with the annual GAR Encampment held in June. The GAR, or Grand Army of the Republic, was a fraternal organization composed of veterans of the Union Army who served in the Civil War.

Most if not all of these ancestors were in some way affiliated with the city's Commercial Club, an early precursor to today's chambers of commerce.

A possible additional inspiration came prior to 1921 in the form of a series of annual motor boat races held on the Willamette River as part of an event known as the Newberg Regatta. The gala featured a parade, a queen contest and a dance.

The Newberg Berry/Berrian Festival featured a "Grand Parade," presenting the queen with the keys to the city, a queen's coronation, races and stunts, a baseball game, a grand tug of war, water fights, free berries and cream at booths on First Street, speeches, and a Berrian Band concert at Wood-Mar Hall at Pacific College, now George Fox University.

In later years, activities were added such as ballet dancing, fireworks, a water regatta on the Willamette River and the Berrian Ball.

In keeping with its overall mission to promote Newberg, the Berrians enjoyed taking their "show" on the road, that is, entering a float, a band and drill team in the bigger parades of the Willamette Valley and at the State Fair in Salem.

A particular source of pride among members was the annual invitation to supply a float to the Rose Festival parade in Portland. Over the years, Newberg's entry won numerous prizes.

During the 1930s, dignitaries of the Portland Rosarians returned the favor by participating at the invitation of the Berrians in the royal procession to escort the festival queen to her throne.

The Berrian president was known as the "Chief Blackcap." Other titles for officers had names even more colorful: the vice-president was known as the "Sub-Chief Munger"; secretary, "Chief Scribe Logan"; assistant secretary, "Assistant Scribe Evergreen"; treasurer, "Gold Dollar Keeper of the Patch."

The second Berry Festival was held July 8, 1922. As it continued into the 1920s and then resumed in the later 1930s, the date for the event began to appear on calendars during various weekends in June. Later in the decade, the name transitioned to "Berrian."

From 1928 to 1936, the Berrians were not active and no Berrian Festival was held. The reason, surprisingly enough, centered on the need for new drill team uniforms and being told by the manufacturer that matching material to make the uniforms was no longer available.

By 1937, the organization was active once again and the festival returned. In 1941, members put their full support behind a new event called the Newberg Farm Product Show. It was held in September. Over the next few years, as the show expanded to look more and more like today's Old Fashioned Festival, it became a three-day fete known as the Newberg Berrian Farmeroo.

In 1956, for financial reasons, the Berrians decided to drop the farm products aspect of the event and change the name back to the former Newberg Berrian Festival. This continued until 1975 when the Berrian organization disbanded due to lack of interest.

From 1975 to 1977 the city was without a summer celebration and in 1978, the retail committee of the Newberg Chamber of Commerce held its first Old Fashioned Days.

In 1981, this became the Old Fashioned Festival. And so it remains. ❖

That added "metropolitan appearance"

Known as the Dixon Building when it was built in the summer of 1927 at 516 E. 1st Street, this address is one of only two downtown properties listed on the National Register of Historic Places. The other is the Union Block Building. In September 2014, Dixon housed the Critter Cabana pet store.

Before Critter Cabana, it was Chehalem Mercantile, later Khron's Appliances. There were others.

And before all of these, spanning the years 1927-1980, this was a J.C. Penney Company department store.

The building itself was built and owned by Elmer P. Dixon and Ralph Butt, who then leased it to Penneys. The contractor was S.E. Watkins.

A major reason for its listing on the NRHP is that the J.C. Penney Company was the first nationwide chain department store to enter the local market. The year 1927 was also the 25th anniversary of the giant dry goods retailer, which celebrated the event by opening 112 stores nationwide, including this one in Newberg.

The grand opening was Aug. 19-20, 1927. Prices were so cheap a shopper could buy an entire wardrobe for 20 bucks. Socks brought two bits. Shirts were 79 cents. Overalls cost $1.15. Hats for the ladies ranged from 98 cents to $1.98. Four dollars bought a pair of solid leather shoes.

The Penney company had been founded by James Cash Penney (1875-1971) on April 14, 1902, in Kemmerer, Wyo. He was the son of a Missouri Baptist preacher and 27 years old at the time.

Kemmerer is located 52 miles north of Evanston, Wyo., in the southeastern part of the state. The town is isolated and far from any major cities, so it seems the most unlikely place in the world to witness the birth of one of America's largest retail chains.

An Oregon Trail spur went through Kemmerer. Kemmerer was also home to the finest bootleg whiskey made during the Prohibition years (1920-1933). Much of it was transported to Chicago via the Transcontinental Railroad, which ran right through the center of Evanston.

Penney called his first store The Golden Rule. His initial investment was $2,000.

By the time Penney arrived in Newberg, there were 33 other stores operating in Oregon. So the brand was known and popular.

Newberg was assigned store number 818, in a national network that enjoyed 885 outlets. Total sales throughout this growing empire topped $115 million in 1926, up $28 million from the previous year. In an age without shopping malls or television advertising, this was an extraordinary level of financial success. Around Newberg newspapers and word-of-mouth carried the message.

In the 1920s, the opening of a Penney store in a small-town came with the same level of excitement that once accompanied the appearance of a McDonald's in the middle-of-nowhere Kansas.

You sense it in that first story done by the *Graphic* on July 14, 1927, announcing the opening:

"The addition…will be a distinct advantage to Newberg people and gives the commercial section of the city an added metropolitan appearance."

When new, the main floor was 40-by-104 feet, with a 24-by-10 mezzanine in the rear for additional retail. A balcony was situated above the big show windows at the front of the building and provided space for the head cashier and an office for the store manager. Throughout, the fixtures of solid oak were made in Grand Rapids, Mich.

From the original appearance of the building, the front and rear entrances have been altered. Skylights, which adorned the interior, have been removed or covered up.

This above-below floor arrangement followed a cookie-cutter interior footprint becoming increasingly popular with the company.

Terms were cash-and-carry and prices never fluctuated. Penney did not do sales or seasonal discounts.

By 1927, Newberg was beginning to boom as a town.

Almost 25 new businesses and public and private buildings had been opened in the downtown area in the previous six years.

In addition, the town had a new Spaulding Paper & Pulp Company plant under construction. Numerous streets had been paved, including many in the central part of town. River and Wynooski streets were two of these. Within the city limits, 27 new houses had been built.

It's little wonder Penney executives picked this moment to break into the Newberg market.

All this growth, of course, was good for newspapers. The *Graphic* began to enjoy unprecedented profits for its owners, Chet Dimond and William Nottage, who had taken over the paper in 1921. With the new Penney account, the *Graphic* announced in September it would soon be moving to a new building at 109 N. School Street.

The town greeted Penney with open pocketbooks. Manager A.E. Lathrop was thrilled.

The weather gave its own welcome.

On Tuesday, Sept. 6, rain rose above the sidewalks on E. First. Shoppers stayed home. Two days later, Lathrop joined other business owners in demanding the Newberg City Council build a better drainage system.

J.C. Penney left Newberg in 1980. Shopping mall locations had become popular, signaling for national chains the end of downtown locations as a viable business model.

The space stayed vacant until August 1981 when a women's clothing store, Fine n' Foxy, and a restaurant, the McMinnville-based The Sage Restaurant, enjoyed a double occupancy of the space. The clothing store was a relocation of the business from a South College address. The restaurant specialized in soup and sandwiches. ❖

The uncorking of Newberg

J ust before Christmas in the year 1912, over two dozen volunteers from the protestant churches of Newberg went door to door to inventory church affiliation.

Of the 2,036 people they surveyed, only 20 were vague in their affiliations. One can only imagine the role Christian morality played a century ago in teaching our town how to keep itself in check.

And no subject generated more teachings than the evils of booze.

By 1900, Newberg was already a well-known stronghold for the Women's Christian Temperance Union. Founded in the 1870s, the WCTU was America's first mass organization devoted to using applied Christianity to accomplish a "sober and pure world."

The *Graphic* served as a strong voice for the local WCTU chapter. The paper borrowed its editorial philosophy from the national organization's belief that alcoholism was the cause of larger social issues.

Occasionally the paper did go after the individual drinker, as in the sad case of Perry Warren, age 50. On Aug. 8, 1912, the former real estate agent became the *Graphic's* exhibit No. 1 for illustrating the negative consequences of strong drink.

To help cope with the loss of his wife, Warren had taken to the liquor habit, forcing his brother, a medical doctor, to move him to a three room cabin near Lents, a part of Portland today in the vicinity of Powell Boulevard.

On Tuesday, Dec. 6, Warren had visited with friends and had taken the occasion to have an adult beverage or two. Arriving back at his cabin in an undetermined state, he had decided to relocate a 50-pound box of dynamite stored beneath his bed.

Lifting the box, he lost his grip. The dynamite hit the floor.

The explosion broke windows for half a mile. Neighbors were knocked from their beds. Perry Warren's cabin was blown "over the space of an acre, with no two pieces of lumber left together."

Except for three years in the 1930s, it was illegal to sell alcohol inside the Newberg city limits for almost half a century. By the 1960s, only two towns in Oregon remained dry, this one and Monmouth, 38 miles south in Polk County. We became legal in 1966, Monmouth in 2003.

It's also true it was never illegal to drink alcohol in Newberg; drinkers only had to go outside the city limits to get what they needed.

This dichotomy was the perfect environment for conflict. Long-timers still refer to it as Wet-Dry Wars.

By the end of the 1880s, the controversy was fully in the open.

The drys took comfort with such *Graphic* editorials as this one, from Christmas 1888:

"The people of Newberg have said in public mass convention that no honorable man will open a saloon or sell liquor as a beverage in the town. Anyone attempting such a thing will do so knowing that the citizens do not consider him an honorable man. We trust it will be a long time before such a man will come to Newberg."

The drys were also helped by what appears to have been a self-appointed group of "temperance authorities" operating at the turn of the century to help maintain the proper "social order."

This strong moral code against imbibing irritated the wets. Aware of the stigma, they ignored it, often devising ingenious ways of keeping their habits hidden from public view. A few years ago, a home owner of an old "Grubby End" Victorian showed me a hidden compartment beneath the house where empty whiskey and gin bottles could still be seen.

In 1919, Congress passed the National Prohibition Act (informally, the Volstead Act) which outlawed in every state the manufacture, sale and transportation of "intoxicating liquors."

The Newberg drys now had laws at the federal level to back their claims.

Repeal of Volstead by Congress in 1933 quickly led to legislation in Salem making liquor sales in Oregon legal. The law included a provision that towns could remain "dry" if enough voters approved.

Locally, the decision fell on the City Council, with the mayor casting the deciding vote. The sale of liquor became legal. Several taverns opened for business. The wets rejoiced. The drys yelled foul, claiming the council had no right to decide the issue for the rest of the town.

The dispute was settled in 1936. The result: 807 dry votes, 594 wet.

The drys would not be challenged again until 1962, when the Newberg chapter of the United States Junior Chamber of Commerce (Jaycees) entered the fight.

Not only did they prove the town was losing at least $12,000 a year in revenues from liquor taxes and licensing, prohibition was preventing the annexation of property around the city that included a new shopping center near Everest Road.

Another election. The drys won again, by 59 votes.

But the Jaycees were not finished. They pushed facts hard to ignore: there were five taverns operating within 500 feet of the city limits, reminding residents that only the sale of alcohol in Newberg was illegal, not the drinking of it.

The two factions went at it again in 1964, with the drys prevailing by 18 votes.

Sensing victory, the Jaycees in 1966 staged the final showdown.

This time the wets claimed the win by 200 votes. The argument that Newberg was losing much-needed revenue had won the day.

And so it remains.

Oregon state law (ORS 471.045) now makes "dry" communities illegal. ❖

INTERESTING FOLKS

The man who gave us Captain America

Comic book icon Captain America has a local connection in the person of Alex Schomburg, who lived here in Newberg from 1962 until his death in Hillsboro in 1998.

Schomburg is one of the best-known comic book illustrators in the history of the genre.

His artistic skills brought to life such action figures as the Human Torch, the Sub-Mariner, Brick Bradford, Doc Strange, Miss Masque, Alley Oop, Broncho Bill, the Black Terror, Princess Pantha, Judy of the Jungle and the Fighting Yank.

His biggest claim to comic book fame is that he was one of several artists who illustrated Captain America.

His freelanced, often airbrushed illustrations, described by collectors as "wild and amazing," graced the covers of hundreds of comic books for the top publishers in the business in the 1940s, including *Marvel Comics, Wonder Comics, America's Best Comics, Exciting Comics* and *Timely Comics* (a forerunner to *Marvel*).

Schomburg's are highly collectible and easy to identify because he signed them with either his last name, or "Xela," a reverse spelling of Alex. Current examples of his original artwork on eBay sell for upwards of $9,000.

Stan Lee, *Marvel Comics'* editor-in-chief, summed up our famous Newbergian this way: "Alex Schomburg was to comic books what Norman Rockwell was to *The Saturday Evening Post*. When it came to illustrating covers, there simply was no one in Alex's league."

In Ron Goulart's *Comic Book Culture: An Illustrated History*, the author labels Schomburg "the undisputed champ of cover artists and the Hieronymous Bosch of comics."

Schomburg was also a prolific science fiction artist, announcing his entry into the field with the September 1939 issue of *Startling Stories*. The endpapers he did for the *Winston Juvenile Series* in the 1950s helped define the art form.

Up to and including the 1980s, his work graced the covers of hundreds of science fiction digest magazines, including *Amazing Stories, Fantastic Universe, Satellite* and Isaac Asimov's *Science Fiction Magazine*.

A native of Aguadilla, Puerto Rico, Schomburg was born on May 10, 1905, and passed away April 7, 1998.

He moved to New York City in the early 1920s, where he began work as a commercial artist with three of his brothers.

In 1928, the family partnership ended and he then created latern slides and movie trailers for the National Screen Service.

He won every major award for science fiction art, as well as comic book art, including a Lifetime Achievement Award at the 1989 Hugo Awards; an Inkpot

Award; the first Doc Smith Lensman Award in 1978; and the Frank R. Paul Award in 1984.

In 1999, he was inducted posthumously into the Eisner Award Hall of Fame at Comic-Con International. This is the Comics Industry's equivalent of the movie industry's Oscar awards.

Those who remember the famous artist recall a quiet man, often seen in his later years walking with his wife along the 600 block of Meridian near their home.

Across the street lived Ron Stansell, who recently told me, "Mrs. Schomburg suffered from Alzheimer's disease and Alex always showed a faithfulness to her that was heartwarming to watch."

According to GFU Director of Public Information Rob Felton, in a feature he wrote for the university's website in May 2013 titled, "Captain America Connection," Schomburg had the opportunity in the 1960s to work with director Stanley Kubrick as he developed the film '2001: A Space Odyssey.' Back home, the artist would occasionally guest-lecture at GFU, especially for English professor Ed Higgins' science fiction class.

"Schomburg would regale us with anecdotes of meeting and knowing Isaac Asimov, Arthur C. Clarke and many of the notable 'founding fathers' of the '40s and '50s pulp era," Higgins told Felton.

"I remember him as being very unassuming–dressed in a cardigan sweater like Mr. Rogers–and I honestly never knew he was so widely known as an illustrator."

Today, GFU owns Schomburg's house just north of Wood-Mar Hall and has converted it into a residence facility for students. A sign with his last name in the front yard marks the exact address. ❖

Death comes to the Van Valins

D eath can come fast or slow.
For Newberg dentist Ralph Waldo Van Valin and his wife, Minnie, death came the fast way, a classic case of being in the wrong place at the wrong time.

Actually, as the two boarded United Airlines Flight 629 in Denver, Colo., in 1955, had they known the fate that awaited them just minutes ahead, they would have wanted it that way.

They were among Newberg's most prominent residents and had lived in Newberg since 1916. They were the parents of an only son and resided at 310 N. College. On this day, Nov. 1, 1955, Dr. Van Valin was celebrating his 72nd birthday.

He was a graduate of North Pacific Dental College in Portland (now OHSU School of Dentistry). Establishing his practice in Newberg, he stayed his entire career and retired in 1953. He was noted around the West Coast for using X-rays in dentistry and often traveled to meetings and conventions to do workshops on the subject.

He was twice Chief Blackcap of the Berrians (sponsors of what would today be the Old Fashioned Festival), and had served as president of the Commercial Club (currently Chehalem Valley Chamber of Commerce), the Rotary Club and the Masons.

He was also a member of the city park board that had established a municipal swimming pool for Newberg. It was located at Hoover Park. His office was at 618 E. First, second floor, the Union Block Building.

A noted genealogist in the state, Minnie Olivia Davis Van Valin was 62. She had authored at least 38 manuscripts tracing the history of early Oregon families and had co-authored the highly-respected *Pioneer Families of Yamhill County* in 1953. She was also a member of the Daughters of the American Revolution and was active in the American Legion Auxiliary.

The three hours the Douglas DC-6B would need to fly them from Denver's Stapleton Airport back to Portland would end a two week vacation the couple had taken at Ralph's Unionville, Pa., birthplace. Minnie had gone on a side trip to Washington, D.C., to do genealogical work.

Conditions were near perfect for a routine flight to the Pacific Northwest. A fresh crew had just boarded to take the plane the rest of the way to its final destination, Seattle.

The new pilot was 39-year-old Lee H. Hall, who had been with United for 14 years and had over 10,000 hours in the air. The first officer was Donald White, age 26, with over 1,000 hours in this particular aircraft. The flight engineer, Samuel

Arthur, was also a veteran of commercial flying and a licensed pilot. All three lived in Seattle. The senior stewardess was Jacqueline Hinds from Eugene.

The four-engine luxury liner was the pride of the United Airlines fleet. It even had its own name, the "Mainliner Denver." It flew the prestigious New York to Seattle route by way of Chicago, Denver and Portland on a routine basis.

With liftoff at 6:52 p.m., a bomb composed of 25 sticks of dynamite planted in Daisie King's luggage by her son, John Gilbert "Jack" Graham, detonated in mid-flight at around 7:03 p.m. Everyone aboard was sent to eternity in a giant fireball.

The victim count totaled 39 passengers and five crew members. The plane, or what was left of it, crashed over a six-mile area, mostly on a beet farm near the town of Longmont, Colo.

The case of Flight 629 remains one of the most bizarre in the history of American aviation. It represented only the second time in U.S. history that a passenger plane had been downed by sabotage over the U.S. mainland. Since then, and except for 9-11, there have only been three others. At that time, it was reported as the largest mass murder in American history.

King, a 53-year-old West Denver businesswoman and restaurateur, was traveling to Alaska to visit a daughter. She was famous for her "broasted chicken" recipe. When not working, she lived with her murderer son and his wife.

Thirteen days after the crash, Graham admitted he had killed his mother so that he could cash in on both her will and a large insurance policy she had taken out in his name. Also, he had purchased life insurance on her at the airport just before her departure.

Later, during his 1956 trial, he recanted. But it was too late. His defense team could not undue the damage of his earlier testimony.

Given the death sentence, Graham was sent to the Colorado State Penitentiary. Soon after, he tried to commit suicide. On the night he was executed, Jan. 12, 1957, he was reported to have been in a jovial mood. As he was being escorted to the gas chamber he was asked if he had any remorse.

None, he said. "I can't help it. Everybody pays their way and takes their chances."

In addition to the Van Valins, *Life* magazine reported that passengers aboard the ill-fated flight included a young couple celebrating their first wedding anniversary, a trustee of Brown University, a Sherwood, Ore., geologist, the widow of a Forest Grove, Ore., minister, a leading nutrition expert on his way to Oregon State College in Corvallis to be a guest speaker, the superintendent of Seattle's humane society, several vacationing stewardesses, and two top executives for Oldsmobile.

The youngest victim in the crash was a 14-month-old infant named James Fitzpatrick. His father was an Army officer stationed on the Pacific island of Okinawa who had only seen his son once. The boy died asleep in his mother's arms. ❖

The Ku Klux Klan in Newberg

As tempting as it is to think Yamhill County enjoys a special isolation from the rest of the world—and I suppose in some ways it does—history tells us otherwise.

This was never more true than in the early years following World War I, when the rebirth of one of America's more sordid chapters in human and cultural relations spread across the country like a rash.

The "rash" called itself the Knights of the Ku Klux Klan. Historians sometimes refer to it as the "second" Klan, to distinguish it from the original KKK, which was born in Tennessee just after the Civil War and had faded from influence and visibility by sometime in the 1870s.

The second Klan was launched with a cross burning atop Georgia's Stone Mountain in 1915. By 1921, the Knights had a million members. By 1925, the ranks had ballooned to 5 million.

It was especially potent in the rural areas of the South and West. In Oregon, an estimated 14,000 men and women belonged. Every city, town and county was affected.

The Knights of the KKK was an outgrowth of propaganda during World War I that demanded "one hundred percent Americanism." After the war, this emotion could not be immediately turned off and became redirected against racial and ethnic minorities considered "un-American."

Here in the Beaver state, the targets were African-Americans, peoples of Asian descent, Jews and Roman Catholics. Purporting to stand for Christianity, morality and Americanism, the Klan was anything but.

In 1922, the Oregon KKK reached its zenith when it threw the weight of its political might in support of Democrat Walter M. Pierce for governor. Pierce was elected over Republican challenger Ben Olcott.

Flush with victory, the Klan then pushed for the passage of the "Compulsory Education Act." It banned everything except public education, a clear slap in the face of the many Catholic and other parochial and private schools operating in the state. However, before it could be enacted, the act was declared unconstitutional by the Supreme Court.

In Portland, Fred L. Gifford, a Minnesota native, quit his $250-a-month job as a manager for the Northwestern Electrical Co. to take a $600-a-month job as Exalted Cyclops of the local Klan. He soon became Grand Dragon of Oregon, then Deputy Wizard for all states west of the Rockies.

Oregon's local KKK chapters, of which there were approximately 60, were known as "Klans." In Newberg, according to documents held at the Newberg Public Library, meetings were held under the auspices of "Newberg Klan No. 24."

Oregon's KKK women were organized separately and operated under two names: Ladies of the Imperial Empire or LOTIE until 1923, then Women of the Ku Klux Klan or the WKKK.

Newberg's connection to LOTIE is significant.

Buried in Friends Cemetery is Maybelle Bents. Until 1923, and using the name of her second husband, Charles W. Jette, she was the head of LOTIE for the state and was known as "Mother Counselor."

Even today, little is known about the details of her involvement. The fact that the KKK operated in great secrecy and kept limited documents and records serves as an impediment to anyone doing research on its members.

However, thanks to the work of two Portland researchers—Sharie Kelley and Lynn Deal—who are currently co-authoring a book about the women's KKK in Oregon and who graciously shared some of their findings with me, details of Maybelle's life are starting to come together.

She was born in 1888 in Wisconsin, at some point later moving to Portland, where in 1905 she married George Chickering. The union produced two daughters and lasted three years. She then became the wife of Charles Wilfred Jette in 1908. She was his third marriage. The two produced a son.

It was during the last several years of this relationship that she became involved with LOTIE, and it was Maybelle who was serving in the organization's top position when an overthrow of the group by the Knights of the KKK occurred in 1923. The Knights' plan was to do away with LOTIE and replace it with the Women of the KKK.

According to University of Pittsburg Historian Kathleen Bee, in her book *Women of the Klan: Racism and Gender in the 1920s*, the WKKK had been created as a money-making scheme to support Oregon's first family of the Klan, the aforementioned Fred Gifford and his wife, Mae. The take over was violent.

To complete the putsch, Gifford needed the LOTIE charter in his possession. To make sure, he sent Rush Davis of Shreveport, La., to Portland's Redmen's Hall, where a large contingent of LOTIE members had assembled.

Mother Counselor was in attendance, enthroned and surrounded by her bodyguard (known as the Honor Guard). Although Dr. Bee does not mention Maybelle Jette by name, it can be reasonably assumed that she was the "Mother Counselor" involved in what happened next.

Crashing the meeting and demanding the charter be turned over, only to be ignored by the women, Davis physically attacked Mother Counselor. He was immediately surrounded by the Honor Guard, who, according to an eyewitness, "swarmed upon him, pummeling, pounding and hammering him until he began to cry for help."

A policeman passing by heard the commotion and rescued the beaten Davis. Mother Counselor immediately led her triumphant ladies in a verse of the "Star-Spangled Banner."

Despite the commotion, the Gifford and Davis contingents prevailed, got the charter, and LOTIE was no more. It is unclear if Maybelle later became a member of the WKKK.

Now for the rest of her story.

In February 1922, she filed for divorce with Charles. In December 1924 she married again, this time to a Champoeg/St. Paul hops farmer named Henry Louis Bents, a man 28 years her senior. At some later point, they made their home in the Newberg area.

After his death in 1935 (he was 75), she moved to Burley, Idaho, near Twin Falls, where she worked as an advice columnist for the *Burley Herald*. She wrote under the *nom de plume* of Wynn Bentley, which she had derived from her middle name and a variation of her late husband's last name.

She also wrote poems, described as "sentimental," and was a landscape artist.

She married her fourth husband, Homer Patterson, late in the 1930s. By 1943 they were living in Portland and she was employed by the federal government's farm labor office.

After Homer died in the early 1960s, Maybelle moved to Clark County Washington and lived with family members in Vancouver and La Center before settling down at Cherry Stone Senior Citizen Apartments in Battle Ground. When she died, she was a resident of the Pythian Home in Vancouver. She left behind children, grandchildren and great- grandchildren. ❖

Hitless Wonder

Let's do a local tribute to the sport of Major League Baseball.

From 1917 to the 1960s, Newberg was home to William Joseph "Billy" Sullivan (1875-1965), whose career in professional baseball spanned the years 1899 to 1916, first with the Boston Beaneaters (1899-1900), then the Chicago White Sox (1901-1914), and finally with the Detroit Tigers (1915-16).

Born on Feb. 1, 1875, in Fort Atkinson, Wis., Billy died in Newberg on Jan. 28, 1965, a few days short of his 90th birthday. His debut behind the plate was on Sept. 13, 1899; his final game was played April 15, 1916.

After settling down on a 20-acre farm at the corner of Sullivan Lane and North Valley Road four miles west of Newberg, Sullivan made his living first with apples, then walnuts and finally with filberts. Billy had grown up on a farm so the lifestyle was familiar. He named his spread the "Home Plate Orchard" and would remain here the rest of his life.

Originally, Sullivan's orchard was supposed to be a partnership involving three former big leaguers: Sullivan; teammate Fielder Jones, who also served as head baseball coach at Oregon Agricultural College in 1910; and Joseph Tinker, of the Chicago Cubs' famous "Tinker to Evers to Chance" combination.

It was to be called "The White Sox Orchard" (featured next in this section), however, nothing ever came of it. Although Jones did get involved but without ever moving to Newberg, Tinker, for whatever reason, declined.

Bart Murdock, a neighbor and baseball historian, told the *Graphic* in 2001 that he had once heard that the "White Sox Orchard" was originally the idea of Sox manager Clark Griffith, who had purchased 10 parcels of land in the Chehalem Valley to be delved out at some future point to favorite White Sox team members. "But there was never a fruition of the plan," he said. "There's no sign that anyone other than Jones and Sullivan ever showed up in Newberg."

Sullivan raised two sons at Home Plate Orchard, Joseph and "Billy Jr." The house still stands. Billy Jr. played in the major leagues from 1931-47 and was, like his father, a catcher.

After his first wife died in 1933, Billy Sr. married Myrtle Nash. Friends of the couple remember her as always referring to her husband as "Mr. Sullivan."

Sullivan would achieve his greatest fame as the starting catcher for the White Sox in the 1906 World Series, the first-ever involving two teams from the same city. The Cubs had won an extraordinary 116 games that year, a major league record that would stand until 2001 when the Seattle Mariners tied it. No one gave the Sox a chance, primarily on the fact that the team had finished the '06 campaign with the lowest batting average in the American League.

In fact, baseball statisticians could look all the way back to 1876 and find no other major league team that had ever won a pennant with as low a team batting average as the Sox's .230 mark. This prompted sportswriters to dub them the "The Hitless Wonders."

In six games, Sullivan, manager Fielder Jones, and the rest of their teammates made the impossible look easy by defeating the Cubs four games to two. The feat remains as one of the greatest upsets in professional sports history.

Additional interesting facts about Sullivan's career:

-He left home at age 22 to seek his baseball fortune.
-He spent two years in the minors, with Dubuque and Columbus.
-He began his career with the Boston Braves in 1899 and was paid $1,000.
-The year he signed with the White Sox, 1901, they won the pennant.
-He played and managed in the majors for 15 seasons.
-In his first major league at-bat, he faced Cy Young and got a hit.
-In 1906, Sullivan led the White Sox in homers with two four-baggers.
-He caught every game of the 1906 World Series.
-He played in 1,141 games.

No discussion of Sullivan is complete without a mention of an antic he and teammate Ed Walsh tried on Aug. 10, 1910. With the future Hall of Fame pitcher standing atop the Washington Monument some 500 feet above the ground, 23 baseballs were dropped straight down to a waiting Billy Sullivan, who figured he would have little difficulty snagging most of them.

He was wrong.

A stiff wind was up that day and played havoc on the balls, whipping most of them away from Sullivan's waiting mitt to fall harmlessly to the ground. One story, published in the *Graphic* in 2001, says Sullivan ended up catching not a single one. However, in his obituary in the *Graphic* a few days after his death, it was stated that "he gained a measure of fame as the first person ever to catch a baseball thrown from the top of the Washington Monument."

The obit went on to say that "in addition to his athletic prowess, he invented the first modern catcher's chest protector and introduced to the game the present catcher's position directly behind the batter. Before his time, catchers normally stood 10 to 20 feet behind the plate."

When son Billy Jr. played in the 1940 World Series as a catcher for the Detroit Tigers, the two, Sr. and Jr., became the first father-son pair to have played in a Series.

Later in life, Sullivan loved the opportunity to speak in public and was often asked to do so. He was very prominent among walnut and hazelnut growers in the area and was highly visible at St. Peter's Catholic Church in Newberg, where he was a member of the Knights of Columbus. He also belonged to the Elk's Lodge in McMinnville, which honored him with a lifetime membership just before his passing.

Suffering a heart attack on Wednesday, Jan. 27, 1965, he was rushed to Newberg Community Hospital. He died of heart failure at 4:30 a.m. the next morning, a few days short of his 90th birthday and the last surviving member of the Hitless Wonders. He was taken to St. James Cemetery in McMinnville for burial. Over 300 attended the service, including many dignitaries from professional baseball.

After his death, Myrtle moved out of the house and into the home of neighbor Ernie Simantel, who had built an apartment for her to stay in. In 1974, Donald and Toni Boyer bought the Sullivan house. The 2012 Yamhill County phone directory had a listing for Donald still at this address. ❖

White Sox Orchard

The year Billy Sullivan's team beat the Chicago Cubs to claim the '06 world title, the White Sox manager was Fielder Jones, who also played center field for the Sox. Today, we would call him a player/manager.

Jones retired from the diamond in 1909 and moved to Portland, where he had started his professional baseball career in the 1890s.

His return to the Rose City was to accept an offer to serve as president of the Northwestern League, a minor league affiliation involving teams from Portland (Cubs), Seattle (Turks), Spokane (Indians), Tacoma (Tigers) and a few others.

And as we saw in the previous feature, Jones also coached at Oregon Agricultural College (now OSU) in Corvallis in 1910.

At this time, his interest in the Beaver state had grown to include considerable holdings in timber and in Yamhill County agribusiness.

One of his investments was a partnership with two other ballplayers in a fruit orchard west of Newberg. It would be the location where the former catcher would eventually settle and spend the rest of his life.

One partner was Jones. The other in the triumvirate held the most fame.

He was Joe Tinker himself, a member of the most famous double play tandem in baseball history, Tinker to Evers to Chance.

Tinker played for the Chicago Cubs as shortstop from 1902-1912. He hailed from Kansas but cut his teeth in the sport when he competed with the Portland Webfoots baseball club for the 1901 and 1902 seasons. Today, he is in the Baseball Hall of Fame.

Years later, as we have seen, Sullivan would call the location the "Home Plate Orchard," but in the beginning the idea was to call it "White Sox Orchard."

There was even some talk of turning the place into some sort of retirement community for former White Sox players.

With the Sox as his archrivals, what must it have taken to talk Joe Tinker into naming the venture, "White Sox Orchard?"

The moment is lost to history.

Jones returned to baseball for a few years before moving back to Portland in 1916. He died there from heart complications in March 1934. Tinker eventually settled in Florida, where he dabbled in managing, scouting and real estate.

There were several others who may have also considered joining these three in the partnership.

Prior to the start of the 1909 major league season, White Sox owner Charles Comisky asked Chicago Tribune Sports Editor Harvey T. Woodruff to go to Portland to see if he (Harvey) could talk Fielder Jones into returning to Chicago to coach the Sox.

Upon arriving, Woodruff was rebuffed by Jones. At the same time, he instantly fell in love with the Pacific Northwest. He vowed that when he retired he would make Oregon his home.

Hearing of Woodruff's failure, Comisky decided to play hard ball. He sent Ban Johnson, founder and president of the American League, to find Jones. Ban had no more success than his predecessor. Did he too fall in love with the state and want to relocate here?

Closing out his feature story on these major leaguers in the May 2, 1912, edition of the *Graphic*, writer A. Phanne commented:

"And who knows that baseball is eternal. Kingdoms rise and fall; races of men wax and disappear; but sun and rain and soil have been in partnership from the beginning. And strangers, gazing in admiration at the White Sox Orchards shall think the name comes from the trimly painted tree-trunks, shinning white above the dark rich ground."

Don't ya just love the way newspapers were written back in the day? ❖

The "Voice of Experience"

Before there was a Dr. Laura (Schlessinger) or a Dr. Phil (McGraw) or any of the other scores of pop-psychology personalities in television, radio and the newspapers, there was "Doctor" Marion Sayle Taylor, generally considered a true pioneer in using broadcast media (in his case, radio) to bring the psychiatrist's couch to America's living rooms.

You might think of him as America's first male Ann Landers of the airwaves.

In his day, Taylor was one of the country's best-known broadcast celebrities. Photographs of him are rare and show a smiling, self-confident, slightly balding, wispy-haired man with the world at his fingertips.

He also had strong Newberg and Yamhill County connections, which we'll get to in a minute.

From 1926-1934, using the stage name "The Voice of Experience," the good "Doctor" solaced thousands of uncertain minds over the hundreds of affiliate stations that were members of the CBS radio network. His style was often described as "homespun," to suit the simple tastes of his massive following.

He was sponsored by Wasey Products, a manufacturer of hair tonics, plus certain other medications concocted to relieve the symptoms of stomach acidity. So successful were his booming voice and "clean handling" of every imaginable problem associated with growing up, relationships and marriage, it took 29 private secretaries, all male, to answer his correspondence. At his peak, his mail count reached 6,000 letters a day.

In addition to having hosted over 5,000 broadcasts by 1934, Taylor was a prolific writer of self-help books, including the best-seller, *Stranger than Fiction,* and over 120 pamphlets on such miscellaneous subjects as "Why Be Unique," "Insomnia," "Why Take Your Own Life?," "The Nudist Fad," "Feminine Shapeliness," "War of the Sexes," "Square Pegs in Round Holes," "Promiscuous Kissing," "The In-Law Problem," and "Are You Afraid of Insanity?"

He lived on Manhattan's Park Avenue and had a private gymnasium in his apartment to keep himself fit.

The "Voice of Experience" told his many fans he was born on the Louisville plantation that produced Old Taylor Whiskey, the son of a retired evangelist. In fact, researchers today suggest his birthplace may actually have been Morrilton, Ark. The date was Aug. 16, 1888 or 1889.

After a false start toward the ministry, young Taylor attended William Jewel College in Liberty, Mo. He next enrolled at Pacific University in Forest Grove to seek a medical degree. The dream was abandoned when a traffic accident took away the coordination in his hands necessary for surgery.

The title "Doctor" came at the suggestion of legendary politician and orator William Jennings Bryan (1860-1925), long after Taylor had established his reputation as national adviser to the lonely and lovesick.

Scrupulously ethical in his radio addresses, he never gave medical advice—except to endorse the medicines that sponsored his programs. He adopted "The Voice of Experience" moniker in 1928.

Taylor married a Newberg woman named Pauline Moore, the daughter of Mr. and Mrs. G.W. Moore. Afterwards, he became the principal of the high school in Amity.

Moving and living for a time in McMinnville, he went south to serve as an administrator for schools in North Bend and Marshfield before venturing to California and Hollywood to seek his fortune. At some point, he divorced Pauline and remarried.

His last visit to Newberg occurred in 1938 while he was on a world tour.

During his stay, maybe because he meant it, maybe because he was used to telling folks what they wanted to hear, Taylor gave credit for his success to Pauline's parents. After entertaining a packed house at an Elks Club benefit, he was gone, never to return.

Early in life he was a proficient organist and was guest organist at the St. Louis World's Fair of 1904. The same automobile accident that took away his dream of becoming a real medical doctor forced him from the keyboard into other lines of work.

He was also nationally known for his private charity work. From his own pocket he paid for innumerable funerals, bought wooden legs and glass eyes, and helped hundreds of listeners with their past-due rent. In 1934 alone he paid for 413 blood transfusions and the hospital bills of 583 unwed mothers.

Taylor died of a heart attack in Hollywood on Feb. 1, 1942. He was 54. News of his death made the front page of the *Graphic* on Feb. 5, 1942. ❖

"You're not from around here, are ya?"

In the days of long ago, a popular Newberg pastime was to keep track of the comings and goings of visitors.

Newspaper reporters would frequently visit Newberg's several hotels to inquire about out-of-town guests. The names would then be published, along with whatever the reporter could learn about why the visitor was here. Readers loved it.

Occasionally, someone of particular interest would show up and put the town in a frenzy.

Two favorites are from the year 1912.

The man who memorized the Bible

On Jan. 25, 1912, the *Graphic* reported a visit to town by one William Frederick Jr., a traveling salesman for a large flour plant in Duluth, Minn.

According to the report (backed by Mr. Frederick himself), this enterprising flour salesman told everyone he was the only person in history to memorize the Bible. The whole thing. One supposes that staring at flour all day can do this to a person.

The story continued: "Though not being of any particular church, he can repeat any passage from Genesis to Revelation, and (also) state where it is found.

"His object in doing so is not for the purpose of arguing Scripture, or making a display of his wonderful knowledge along that line, but simply for his own benefit and his love for the Holy Word."

The story is silent on whether anyone took the rare opportunity of his visit to put Mr. Frederick's amazing memory to the test.

World champion "Type Writer"

Then there was a man named H.O. Blaisdell, who had two aunts in Newberg identified only as A.T. Behnke (Mrs.) and L.S. Otis.

In May 1912, Blaisdell came to town to pay his respects.

Now there was nothing unusual about this except that our visitor was the champion of the world in "type writing," a most fitting thing to do since his employer was none other than the Underwood Typewriter Company of New York City.

He was also unusual in that he was a man making a living with a typewriter in an age when almost 85 percent of the users worldwide were women.

Before we proceed, it might be important to explain to our younger readers just what a typewriter is.

According to a popular *Wikipedia* website, "a typewriter is a mechanical or electromechanical device with keys that, when pressed, cause characters to be printed on a medium, usually paper. From their invention in 1868 through much of the 20th century, typewriters were indispensable tools for recording the written word. By the end of the 1980s, word processors and personal computers largely displaced typewriters in the settings where they previously had been ubiquitous in the western world."

Unlike our flour guy, Blaisdell gave demonstrations of his amazing talent at both the high school and the *Enterprise* newspaper, an early rival of the *Graphic*. According to those who saw him, it was "highly entertaining."

How fast was he?

"In the International Contest held in 1910, he won the cup by writing for an hour 6,919 gross words, making 72 errors, which, deducting five words for each error, left him a net rate of 109 words a minute," the *Graphic* said.

"In the 1911 contest, he wrote 7077 words in the hour and, deducting 69 errors, left him a rate of 112 net words a minute, the highest professional record ever made in competition."

To stay in shape, Mr. Blaisdell said he practiced four hours a day. ❖

The famous, the infamous and the downright interesting

The history is Newberg is full of interesting locals. Here's a sampling of some of the folks who jump off the pages of old newspapers and are worth remembering.

David Bishop: Former Newberg police chief who was instrumental in cracking the infamous "I-5 Killer" case in the early 1980s when he was a lieutenant with the Beaverton police department. He was the first to suspect Randall Brent Woodfield of the crimes, the man eventually found guilty of the murders, and sentenced to life in prison at the Oregon State Penitentiary in Salem. After leaving Newberg, he returned to Beaverton as police chief and retired July 1, 2008.

Richard James Foster: Christian author, pastor, George Fox University alumnus (Class of 1964), Dr. Foster is responsible for writing *Celebration of Discipline*, named by *Christianity Today* as one of the Top 10 Christian books of the 20th century. It has sold more than a million copies. He grew up in Garden Grove, Calif. In March 2011, the website *Quaker.com* referred to him as, "The best known Quaker in the world today."

The Four Flats: A nationally renowned men's vocal quartet from Newberg, the principal members were Harlow Ankeny (baritone), Dick Cadd (bass), Ron Crecelius (lead) and Norval Hadley (tenor). They met as students at Pacific College (renamed George Fox College in 1949) right after World War II and earned their widespread reputation by performing first for Youth for Christ ministries and later for World Vision, where they became known as the World Vision Quartet. Performing for this latter organization, the foursome traveled the globe, particularly the Far East.

Todd Giebenhain: A 1993 Newberg High graduate who majored in theater at Western Oregon University in Monmouth, he moved to Los Angeles in 1996 to become an actor, successfully landing spots in numerous Dodge Hemi commercials airing nationally in the early 2000s and appearing as "Richie" in six episodes of the TV series *Malcolm in the Middle* from 2000 to 2002. Among his numerous other acting credits, he also had a role in the movie *Slackers* (2002) and as "Donny" in two episodes of the TV show, *Crime Scene Investigation* (CSI). He has also had roles for TV in *Chicken Soup for the Soul* (1999) and *Raising Hope* (2010), and for the movies *Going Geek* (2001) and *Gigli* (2003). Giebenhain has been involved in the fight to find a cure for cystic fibrosis.

The "Goat Woman": Her real name was Elizabeth McBroom and for many years she was the most recognizable person on the streets of Newberg. Living in an old truck body on the outskirts of town, wearing rubber inner tubes for shoes and sporting long hair matted and filthy from going months without washing, she was known to locals as the "Goat Woman," not so much on account of her unusual appearance but because she never went anywhere without at least a goat or two by her side. Naturally, someone like Miss McBroom was hard to miss on her almost daily jaunts to and from downtown, but when she did go missing around the latter part of October 1942, the Newberg police department went looking. They found her housed in the Multnomah County jail on a disorderly conduct charge. Concluded the *Graphic* on its report of her discovery: "She is reticent to discuss her past life, but it is known that she is well-educated and especially well-informed on past and current history."

Ginger Lile: The Feb. 5, 2011, issue of the *Graphic* announced the acceptance of longtime high school wrestling pairing official Ginger Lile as a new member of the Oregon Chapter of the National Wrestling Hall of Fame. Lile, a special education teacher for 29 years in the Newberg Public School System, was the first woman in Oregon history to be so honored. In 2010, she was named Woman of the Year by USA Wrestling, the national governing body for wrestling in the United States.

William Homer Maris: A Newberg native, Maris is the composer of Oregon State University's alma mater, "Carry Me Back."

Ironically, Maris received his undergraduate degree from the University of Oregon in 1914. He earned a graduate degree in agriculture at Oregon Agricultural College five years later.

In addition to teaching and pursuing a graduate degree through OAC's College of Agriculture, the likable Maris spent his spare time composing the song that would bring him both instant fame and an enduring legacy. Early drafts of the tune were rehearsed at a Corvallis barbershop. It was an instant hit on campus and adopted in 1918 as the school's official song.

After graduation, Maris joined the Army and was sent to the Letterman Hospital in San Francisco to work as a laboratory assistant. In September 1926, he was residing in Oak Harbor, Wash., where he worked as a farmer.

In the fall of 1930, he took an instructor's position at the University of Puget Sound. Returning from an Orpheus Club concert on his bicycle shortly after midnight on the evening of July 23, 1933, Maris was struck by an automobile and killed. ❖

What Ken and Joan Austin did for dentistry

Much has been written and said about Joan Austin to mark the passing (June 5, 2013) of this most amazing and most successful and generous businesswoman. Clearly, in the history of Newberg and Yamhill County, there has never been anyone like her.

In this column, I want to add my own tribute to Joan's life with a story about what she and husband Ken did for dentistry. After all, the two co-founded and co-owned A-dec, one of the world's largest manufacturers of dental equipment.

It's a story as big as what Bill Bowerman did for tennis shoes, what Miles Lowell Edwards did for heart valves, what Pat Casey has done for baseball at OSU.

It speaks to Joan's legacy in ways which extend far beyond the boundaries of this town or state or even this country.

Call it a global legacy, which it is, and it began right after Thanksgiving 1966.

The Austins had been in business for about two years, operating at that time out of a small Quonset hut on Blaine Street.

In addition to developing new products, hiring employees, battling the need for more work space, and raising two children, the couple had to find time to showcase their product-lines to the doctors they hoped would buy them. This meant traveling to trade shows and dental conventions in places like Las Vegas, San Francisco, Dallas and New York City, where our Thanksgiving story takes place.

So far, sales had been scattered. Staying upbeat was important and Ken and Joan had kept their levels high by designing a mobile work station putting small instruments and supplies at the fingertips of a *seated* dentist or an assistant. They called it a Tray-Cart.

In 1966, the concept of a dentist "sitting while working" was a growing trend in the profession. Not only did a person receive better care, sitting (instead of standing) added years to a doctor's career.

A-dec's carts were just the right size and height for the increasing number of dentists recognizing the all-around benefits of the new concept. Joan suggested colors for the carts, another industry first. In the final analysis, the Tray-Cart was twice as functional as the competition. The two had developed the better mousetrap.

Trouble began as soon as the shipping crates with the Tray-Cart samples arrived at the New York City hotel ballroom where the trade show was being held.

"A union representative told me I wouldn't be able to unpack the boxes myself," Ken remembered in a 2005 interview. "I was going to have to hire a union carpenter to do the work."

Ken told the representative, "That may be so, but I built these boxes and I'll open them."

The union man replied, "Here's some advice. If you want your equipment around, you'd better find a carpenter. He doesn't have to do anything, but you still have to have one."

So Ken and Joan paid the $50 union fee (for the carpenter) and moved on. Ken also got to unpack the carts.

More trouble developed at their assigned booth. Their location put them near the entrance to a stairwell accessed by a door. When the door was open, their space was cut in half.

And it probably didn't help that their clothes held the slight odor of printer's ink. Rushing to have product literature printed before leaving Newberg, they had packed it wet. The smell lingered all the way to the show.

Still, they had one more tribulation to endure. Surrounded on all sides by the giants of dental manufacturing, they were approached by three executives of a company atop the industry's pecking order. Looking at A-dec's display of dental carts, one of them remarked:

"They're cute, but they'll never sell."

Such a comment, so arrogantly stated, might have been devastating to a lot of young entrepreneurs. But not the Austins. Instinct told them they had a good thing…and they were right! In 2013, at least 100 dental companies have come and gone and A-dec still sits at the top of its industry.

A-dec's rise to success isn't so much a story of a few great events as it is a story of smaller ones that take on added importance as they accumulate.

What is certain is that Ken and Joan got their start at a time when the dental profession was undergoing fundamental change. Dentists were in the market for delivery systems more compact, more accessible and more convenient than anything previously available. Disappearing were the elaborate units and dental chairs with conventional headrests and footboards that had been the mainstays of the dental office for decades.

Ken and Joan understood these emerging new preferences and used the insights to develop products to match. Between 1966 and 1970, A-dec became the world's first dental manufacturer to give dentists a full range of choices in equipment for *sit-down* dentistry. In doing so, they gave legitimacy to the approach to patient care that has dominated the profession ever since.

The enterprising couple, with Joan often taking the lead in determining how change would impact their business, also became the most savvy at realizing it was the doctors who were triggering new developments within dentistry. In other words, ideas for new products, or modifying existing ones, now flowed backwards from the dentist to the equipment maker.

The trade show became the conduit for the exchange. A-dec used these opportunities to help dentists solve problems, and in doing so, reshaped the world of dental equipment manufacturing. The carts they took to New York were in step with the times, regardless of snide remarks leveled at them by competitors.

For the record, Ken Austin was the first Benny Beaver student mascot for Oregon State University in the early 1950s. ❖

132

The ironman of Newberg

In the annals of sports in the state of Oregon, one of the very best stories we have concerns a football game played on Oct. 21, 1933, featuring the Oregon State College Beavers and the University of Southern California Trojans. The place was Portland's Multnomah Stadium, now Providence Park (names from the past: Jeld-Wen Field, PGE Park, Civic Stadium, Multnomah Stadium).

Newberg, as it happened, has a very special connection to this magical moment.

Trojan Head Coach Howard Jones (1925-1940, 121-36-13) had brought to Oregon over 80 players, plus a portfolio of gridiron success the envy of every coach in the country.

He was riding a 25-game winning streak. Since 1931 he had won back-to-back Pacific Coast Conference championships, Rose Bowls and national championships. He was the Nick Saban of his generation.

His line-up featured three All Americas and numerous All Conference players. Among them was the best defensive lineman in the country, Aaron Rosenberg, one day to be a member of the College Football Hall of Fame and a Hollywood movie producer whose credits include *The Glenn Miller Story* (1954), *The Benny Goodman Story* (1956) and *Mutiny on the Bounty* (1962).

Against five opponents that season, the Men of Troy had scored 141 points and allowed but a single touchdown.

On the opposite side of the ball, Oregon State College's Lon Stiner had 37 players, mostly unknowns, but with a healthy understanding of what they were up against.

Out of that group, Stiner had 11 athletes he especially liked. On this day, he would do something that would make them immortal. He would use no substitutes. The starters would play both offense and defense for 60 minutes.

This was David verses Goliath, Popeye without his spinach fighting Bluto. And as these things often go, the little guy won. More or less. The final whistle blew a 0-0 tie.

Now before you ask yourself what's the big deal, remember that this game is the only game in NCAA history in which a team using no substitutes halts the winning streak of a defending national champion.

Known to Beaver Nation as the "Ironmen" or "Iron Immortals," the 11 who played that day also share another claim to fame. That same season, the group invented "The Pyramid Play," in which a teammate was lifted in the air to block extra point and field goal attempts.

A photo of the "Pyramid," taken at the '33 Civil War game, went viral and forced the NCAA to ban use of the play. The rule is still in effect.

One of the Ironmen was Vernon Wedin (pronounced "Wadeen"), a lineman, who also happened to be the shortest man among the starters.

In July 1936, Wedin was hired as athletic director at Newberg Union High, a position that included both teaching and coaching responsibilities. Born in Minnesota in 1910, he had moved with his parents to Gresham when he was an infant

Not only did he instruct students in general science, he was head coach of four varsity sports: football, basketball, baseball and track. Wedin was also the faculty adviser for the lettermen's club, known at that time as the Order of the "N."

Taking over a program that hadn't won a football game since 1932, the Tigers finished the 1936 season at 3-1-3. The town was thrilled.

Interviewed by telephone from his winter home in Quartzsite, Ariz., 90-year-old and former Newberg Tiger Loren "Tex" Mardock remembered some of the qualities about his coach that made for instant success.

"He was tough and worked the devil out of us," he said. "He knew what had to be done and we did it."

At the same time, Wedin was a "good man," Mardock added, and said his coach was not the kind of person who needed intimidation to keep players motivated.

"He did not ride us. When we did something wrong he told us, but he didn't get on our backs."

Highlighting Wedin's second year was the formation of the Girls' Athletic Association, the first-ever such organization for the school's women athletes. In two years, participation in women's athletics at the school nearly doubled.

The start of the 1939 football season, Wedin's fourth and final year in Newberg, was extraordinary by anyone's standards. Through five games the Tigers were undefeated and had not given up a single point.

Then came what the students referred to as "The Crash," losses to Hillsboro and Beaverton by considerable margins. A win over McMinnville was followed by two more losses to end the season at 6-4.

Marrying NUH physical education teacher and tennis coach Clara Ruff, Wedin and his wife finished the 1939-40 school year and moved to Chehalis, Wash. Here they both taught at the high school, parented three children and stayed the rest of their lives.

He eventually became a vice principal, was promoted to assistant superintendent of schools and passed away in 1971 while still in the position. ❖

Newberg's "Renaissance Man"

Newberg is linked to Shakespearean drama in the mining camps of Idaho, the manufacture of the first dry plates for photography in Oregon history, the formation of the world-famous Mazamas mountaineering club, the development of Government Camp on the shoulder of Mt. Hood, and the building of that popular ski resort's first hotel.

All of these achievements were tallied by the extraordinary Oliver C. Yocum, a "Renaissance Man" if there ever was one. Lucky for us, he lived in Newberg long enough for us to claim him as one of our own.

Indeed, his love for this part of Yamhill County was so strong, he moved back to nearby Dayton to live out his final years (with his wife Ann), spending his leisure time teaching himself to read the Greek Bible.

Known as "O.C." to family and friends, Yocum was five years old when he accompanied his parents, Jesse and Minerva Cooper Yocum, to the Pacific Northwest via the Oregon Trail in 1847.

Reaching Yamhill County, the Yocums lived as gypsy settlers for the next 10 years, moving first to Grande Ronde, then Bellevue and finally Lafayette, where Oliver, now 16, took a job clerking for Morris Wolf, later Sidney Smith.

A restlessness settled on the young man so he moved to Portland. At Sherlock & Co. he learned harness and saddle making. In his spare time, he worked on a deficiency in formal schooling by studying law and the classics. He also developed an interest in Shakespeare, committing to memory many of the Bard's plays.

In 1865 he put his new talent to use by joining a troupe of actors working the mining camps of Idaho. They performed burlesque Shakespeare, which was spreading like wildfire across the West.

Every camp had a stage. Once the curtain lifted, the diggers watched the Bard's plays altered to be less intense, more ludicrous, occasionally ribald, and full of clever comedy and themes that mirrored their own lives.

Tiring of the lifestyle and low pay of a traveling actor, Yocum said goodbye to Shakespeare in 1870 and returned to Lafayette. He married Ann Robertson, moved to Newberg and began farming 50 acres on the northwest part of the J.B. Rogers Donation Land Claim.

In "A Century to Remember," historian Doris Jones Huffman pinpoints the location as "a present-day tract of land on Fifth Street, between Lincoln and Grant streets, continuing south past Dayton Avenue to Ninth Street."

In addition to farming, Yocum was Newberg's best saddle maker and served the area for a time as a Justice of the Peace.

In 1878 he moved to Dayton and two years later was in Portland working as a photographer for I.G. Davidson at First and Yamhill.

In 1882 he moved to the Mt. Tabor neighborhood, set up his own photo gallery, and manufactured what are thought to be the first dry plates for photography in Oregon.

Now a new love entered his life, one that would bring him lasting fame... mountain climbing.

Ascending to the top of Mt. Hood with camera in tow, he became one of the first (if not the first) to take pictures from the summit. He now belonged to the mountain.

In 1890, he began looking for a place close by to live. He found just the spot on a lovely piece of ground adjacent to the old Barlow Road. Today we know the location as Government Camp.

Yocum platted parts of his claim in blocks, naming the streets Yule, Olive, Church, Union and Montgomery...YOCUM. Establishing a post office for the new community, he applied for the name Government Camp but was refused. Pompeii, however, was accepted, but was short-lived.

On July 19, 1894, he was among the 105 climbers who became charter members of the Mazamas, the Pacific Northwest's most prestigious and oldest mountaineering fraternity. The word is from the Nahuatl language of Mexico and means "mountain goat." Membership is reserved for those who have climbed to the summit of a mountain with at least one glacier.

From this point forward, Yocum was one of Hood's top guides.

Today, Mt. Hood landmarks are named in his honor. Hikers enjoy the remote and difficult Yocum Ridge Trail, a 16 mile round trip at 3,600 feet in elevation. The journey begins at the Ramona Falls trailhead and ends at Yocum Meadow. On lovely Camp Creek off Hwy 26, Yocum Falls greets visitors

In July 1909, *Graphic* Associate Editor W.C. Woodward visited O.C. and Ann at their mountain resort and was taken to the top of Hood. Afterwards, Woodward could proudly count himself a true Mazama.

To maximize the experience of what the mountain offered, Yocum in 1899 built the area's first hotel, a 16-room, two-and-a-half story place known as the Mountain View House. The cost was $23,000, an enormous sum for the time.

To protect his investment, he stayed at the facility year-round, even in the dead of winter, when conditions made it impossible for anyone to travel to the area.

In 1910, he sold the property to Elijah Coleman who changed the name to the Government Camp Hotel. On Oct. 11, 1933, the building burned to the ground.

In 1911, at age 69, Yocum gave up his career as a guide and became an assistant chemist at North Pacific Dental College in Portland.

Six years later, he retired from the position and moved to Dayton, where he passed away on March 12, 1928. Ann joined him on July 6, 1931. ❖

A full life, and then some

One of the more interesting aspects of Newberg's history centers on the role transplants have played in the founding and development of our city. Ewing Young, whose arrival just west of Newberg in 1834 helps mark the beginning of non-indigenous settlement of the Willamette Valley, was from Tennessee. Joe and Mary Hess (a. 1843) traveled here from Arkansas.

"Father of Newberg" Jesse Edwards (a. 1880) called Indiana home. A-dec co-founder Joan Austin was born and raised through childhood in the state of Minnesota. Current Newberg mayor Bob Andrews is from Idaho. You get the point.

Which leads to Scott Leavitt, yet another transplant and someone lost to our institutional memory, save for a small city park named in his honor at 1310 E. 10th Street.

Our "Grubby End" honoree lived a full life, and then some.

Born in 1879 in Elk Rapids, Mich., Leavitt's parents were originally from the state of Maine, where father Roswell had been a member of the state legislature.

After relocating to Michigan, Roswell served successfully as a state senator, prosecuting attorney and circuit court commissioner. As we shall see, his career in public service influenced his son and helped determine the young man's future.

While attending high school, Scott enlisted in the 33rd Michigan Volunteer Infantry Regiment and was sent in the early months of 1898 to fight in the Spanish-American War.

Under the command of Brig. Gen. Henry Duffield, the 33rd, along with troops from Ohio and Massachusetts, helped guard the Army's supply depot at the Sibony Beachhead during the Battle of San Juan Hill (July 1, 1898). Leavitt also fought in the Battle of Aguadores.

After his discharge, he enrolled in the liberal studies program at the University of Michigan.

In 1901, he moved to Oregon and bought a farm near Falls City. On Oct. 3, 1903, he married Oregonian Elsie Frink.

Elsie's sister, Bertha Graham, lived in Newberg. Brothers Leonard and Ennis Frink did as well. Given their frequent visits here to visit family, Newberg became a second home to the Leavitts.

From 1901 to 1906, Scott was principal of schools in Falls City, North Yamhill, Dayton and Lakeview.

In 1907, he became one of the first forest rangers with the U.S. Forest Service in the Fremont National Forest (now Fremont-Winema N.F.) in Lake and Klamath counties. Later assignments included stints in Minnesota and Montana.

In 1922, and as a member of the Republican Party in Montana, he was elected to the U.S. House of Representatives. His career in Congress would span four terms (until 1933). His many assignments included serving as chairman of the Committee on Indian Affairs.

Around 1930, he and Elsie became good friends to President and Mrs. Herbert Hoover and were frequent visitors to the White House. With Hoover's connections to Newberg, the relationship was a natural.

Following Leavitt's unsuccessful bid at re-election to Congress in 1932, the couple returned to Montana, after which he became a delegate to the 1932 Republican National Convention. In 1934, he failed in an attempt to gain a seat in the U.S. Senate.

In 1935, he again returned to the Forest Service, this time in Wisconsin, where he would stay until his retirement from forestry work in 1941.

In 1936-37, Leavitt served as commander-in-chief of the National Encampment of United Spanish War Veterans. This was a highly prestigious honor that brought him much recognition throughout the country.

Around the start of World War II, the Leavitts retired to Newberg, to a house on Hancock Street.

Not content with spending his senior years swatting flies on the front porch or taking afternoon naps, Leavitt rolled up his sleeves and became deeply involved in the life of this community.

He joined the Newberg Rotary Club, later serving as district governor of Rotary, was an honorary member of the Newberg Barracks of World War I Veterans, was active in the Newberg Garden Club, and was a frequent attendee at meetings of the Chamber of Commerce.

He also held memberships in the Masons, the National Association of Retired Civil Employees and was a 30-year member of the Forestry Association.

At the time of his death (at home) on Oct. 19, 1966, at age 87, he was chairman of the Newberg Park Board (now Chehalem Park and Recreation District).

Leavitt is interred at the Willamette National Cemetery in Portland. ❖

"Hamburger Gladys"

This story came to me Feb. 17, 2014 when *Graphic* Managing Editor Gary Allen received an email from Denny and Connie Taylor of Chehalis, Wash. The Taylors told Gary they had lived in Newberg from 1973-84 and that one of their fondest memories had been a small diner located near the intersection of Portland Road (Hwy 99W) and Springbrook Road, about where cars today access the parking lot to the Little Cooperstown "business district."

It was operated by Gladys Auld, aka "Hamburger Gladys," who they described as a "unique lady serving handcrafted burgers with rare customer service." They wondered if Gary might do a tribute story about Gladys.

Gary fondly remembered her and decided a feature might tickle some memories in the community. So he called me. Tickling, after all, is what I try to do with this column. I agreed to give it a go. Not only that, I'm a self-proclaimed hamburger connoisseur.

Right up front, I was told by some of my best go-to sources, longtime residents who remembered Gladys' eats so well you could smell meat frying when they talked to you, that she was going to be a tough nut to crack. She hated publicity. Documentation, they agreed, was going to be hard to find.

Undaunted, I visited the Newberg Public Library, a resource that had never let me down. This time the library let me down. I found no stories, no obituaries, almost nothing in print about Gladys except a few entries in old business directories from the 1970s. Suddenly this project began to feel like Hansel and Gretel looking for the witch's house without the trail of bread crumbs.

As a result, I'm still a bit fuzzy on exactly when Gladys and husband George came here, where they were from, when they entered into business, or when everything finally closed.

It was time for Plan B.

Phone calls to folks who knew her revealed that she had died in Salem in 1992, that George had operated a gas station attached to the diner, and that he had died and left her alone to run both businesses. No one ever remembered the two having employees and no one was able to talk about George with any certainty. Gladys rarely mentioned him.

Some said she was born in Canada, others that she was from England.

They were pretty sure the couple had a son named Durran, a daughter named Margaret Jean, and that they lived on Portland Road within walking distance of the diner, in a house hidden today behind tall shrubbery and situated close to the entrance to the Highway 99W Drive-In theater.

Thanks to the Taylors, retired Fire Chief Al Blodgett, Verne Martin of the Newberg Historical Society and Reference Librarian Denise Reilly, plus a host of others who responded to a Facebook query looking for Newbergians who remembered Gladys, I was able to cobble together enough to write a column.

Many recalled she had a limited menu: hamburgers, potato chips (she heated on her grill), grilled cheese sandwiches (with or without ham) and homemade pie. It was her pies and burgers that especially made mouths water.

The place had no tables; everyone sat on stools at a long lunch counter. A copy of the current newspaper was always around. On the back wall hung the tea and coffee cups brought in by regular customers she would grab to serve their beverages.

The gas station attached to the diner never had more than one location. Many knew it as Auld's Mobile Service Station. The diner operated under three names: Corner Cupboard, The Auld's and Auld's Snack Bar. As we'll see in a minute, it operated at several different spots.

Other memories:

About Gladys...Denny Taylor: "She was a careful and quiet observer of people. She had opinions and was rather formal but very gracious, which could make her seem distant, but never rude. If she did not know you she was cautious until she knew you better. Most of the time she sported a red wig and wore a housecoat. She loved flowers and had a large yard."

About her hamburgers and pies (from Facebook)...

William Rosacker: "The best hamburgers I ever ate. What a treat."

Randy Hohnstein: "To this day, I still use Gladys' hamburger patty making technique. Smashing it and tightening it up around the edges. My family watches me and pokes fun at me."

Jon Cox: "It didn't matter if you walked in with 10 people, she made and served each order one at a time."

Grace Pitts: "You ate there, she would not make food to go."

Rose Marugg: "She used to save my father-in-law the last slice of chocolate cream pie. Told us she was out but produced a slice when he walked in."

Sharon Moore: "Dad said the meringue on the pie was huge."

Jenny Crackenberg: "Cream for the pies was individually whipped by hand with a whisk."

Tips...More than one former customer recalled Gladys hated being tipped. She would either return your money or throw it at you, even if she had to follow you out to your car. She liked verbal praise.

Publicity...She always turned down offers from reporters for interviews.

Two locations...Retired Newberg Fire Chief Al Blodgett remembered, "The first was across from Gumm's Market. The 99W/Springbrook intersection was known for years as Gumm's Corner. The market was where Shari's is today. In those days, 99W was a two-lane highway. Gladys was along the road where US Bank is."

*Gladys' place in history…*Denny Taylor: "Even in the early 80s the world around her was accelerating exponentially, with fast and faster food prep. Real customer service was fading and the blur of life was dizzying.

"At Gladys' place you could leave your watch in the car, take a deep breath, enjoy chatting with friends, reading the local paper and eating a delicious burger and a slice of homemade heaven with fresh whipped cream.

"One could go out there and face the blur again with renewed hope! We miss the refuge she offered us in her little diner." ❖

Burt Brown Barker and the Hoover-Minthorn House

O f all the houses and buildings in Newberg that help define our history, there is one that stands supreme: the Hoover-Minthorn House Museum. Located at 115 S. River Street, Hoover-Minthorn was the first property in our city to be listed on the National Register of Historic Places. That was 38 years ago.

Built in 1881 by "Father of Newberg" Jesse Edwards, it was purchased in 1885 by Henry and Laura Minthorn. Henry and Laura were U.S. President Herbert Clark Hoover's foster parents. From 1885 to 1888, Hoover lived here.

It is also generally considered to be Newberg's oldest surviving house.

This story is familiar to most of us.

What isn't so well known is Dr. Burt Brown Barker's story. Dr. Barker played a significant role in the 1940s and '50s to ensure the future of Hoover-Minthorn. It's time we give this remarkable man his due.

Born of pioneer stock on Nov. 3, 1873, in Waitsburg, Wash. (Walla Walla County), he was but a year old when his parents divorced and forced him to live with an aunt and uncle in Salem, Ore. In his Presbyterian Sunday School class was Herbert Hoover, where the two would begin a lifelong friendship.

Graduating from Willamette University in 1893, Burt Barker became the first Oregonian to enroll at the University of Chicago. He returned home in 1897, taught at McMinnville (now Linfield) College, then entered Harvard Law School in 1898. Other credentials he enjoyed included a Doctor of Laws Degree from Linfield in 1935 and a Doctor of Letters Degree from the University of Oregon in 1964.

Beginning in 1901 and for the next 27 years, he would become successful, and rich, thanks to law practices in Chicago and New York City.

Oregon beckoned once again. With his wife Ella Starr Merrill (they were parents to a daughter named Barbara), Barker "retired" in 1928 and relocated to a stunning Chateau Ferme-style house on Southwest Brentwood Drive on Portland Heights.

For the rest of his life he would devote himself to public and community service. He became a director of the First National Bank of Oregon, was a trustee of the McLoughlin Memorial Association of Oregon City, and held leadership positions with the Portland Art Association, Portland Civic Theater, Catlin School, and the Doernbecher Children's Hospital.

He is remembered most, however, for his efforts to help preserve and promote appreciation for Oregon's history.

Indeed, during his lifetime, Barker, whose quiet dignity was his trademark, was affectionately known as the "grand old man of Oregon history."

Beginning in 1935, Barker traveled to London and accomplished something no one in 265 years had been able to do: make public the archives of the Hudson's Bay Company for scholarly research.

Later, his interest in the HBC and its fur trading outpost, Fort Vancouver (situated on the north shore of the Columbia River directly across from Tomahawk Island near the I-5 bridge), led to his involvement in the restoration of the Dr. John McLoughlin House in Oregon City. McLoughlin was Chief Factor, or manager, of the British-owned outpost from 1824-1845.

Barker was chair of the Lewis & Clark Sesquicentennial celebration, an activity highlighted when he convinced the Crown Zellerbach Corporation to donate the logs for what would become a replica of Lewis & Clark's Fort Clatsop near Astoria.

He was responsible for fundraising and placement of the Jason Lee and John McLoughlin statues in the Capitol in Washington, D.C. He also served on the Oregon Centennial Commission in 1959. Along with daughter Barbara Barker Sprouse, Burt helped preserve several buildings at the Aurora Colony in Aurora.

When in the 1930s UO President Arnold B. Hall appointed him to a vice president's position (public relations), Barker accepted, on the condition that his salary be used to sculpt the *Pioneer Mother* statue, seen today in the Women's Quadrangle on the Eugene campus and dedicated on May 8, 1932.

He served twice as director of the Oregon Historical Society. An outstanding scholar, he wrote or edited several books on Oregon history and was a contributor to the *Oregon Historical Quarterly.*

After the Minthorns left Newberg, their house was purchased by Milton Nicholson. Between 1909 and 1912 (after Nicholson had departed), the appearance of the house was altered. For the next 40 years it would be owned twice by Pacific College. In 1947, Barker organized the Herbert Hoover Foundation to raise support to restore the house and turn it into a museum in honor of Hoover's Oregon boyhood. For Barker, it quickly became a labor of love.

The foundation's roll of officers included Pacific College presidents Levi Pennington (retired) and Emmett W. Gulley. Many of Hoover's friends from around the country donated to the cause.

The restoration, under the meticulous leadership of Barker, was guided by the memories of Nicholson's daughters, Bertha May and Lillian, President Hoover himself, Mary Minthorn Strench, and others. Among the reconstruction highlights, L.S. Skene skillfully carpentered the reopening of the original front porch and moved the woodshed to its original location.

Barker also helped secure much of the furniture and furnishings seen in the house by today's visitors.

Hoover came to Newberg for the dedication, celebrated on Aug. 10, 1955, his 81st birthday. Thousands attended, in one of the most historic days in Newberg's history.

Under the watchful eye of current director Sarah Munro, the Hoover-Minthorn House Museum has been owned and operated by The National Society of The Colonial Dames of America in Oregon since 1981.

Burt Brown Barker passed away on Jan. 29, 1969, at age 95. Ella preceded him in death in 1960. ❖

The Alice Ross story

In September 1952, Newberg saw the arrival of a 42-year-old mother of two named Alice Gaddis Wheeler.

It was the beginning of a relationship between transplant and town that inspires us to this day.

If Oregon is anything, it is a place of rebirth and renewal. And so it was for Alice.

A lifelong member of the Society of Friends, she had been through great personal tragedy and looked forward to the spiritual sustenance this Quaker community and its college would be able to offer.

As we will see, she would receive plenty, give plenty in return.

Her journey to Newberg began in 1947, the year her husband was killed in a hunting accident in Africa. They had been there two years working as missionaries.

His name was Eli Wheeler. She had met him in the 1920s in the tiny town of Haviland, Kan., an educational oasis in the middle of the great American prairie.

Alice was one of 13 children born to Wade and Eletta Gaddis of the Bethany Community of Stevens County, Kan., just east of the current Cimmeron National Grassland and legendary "Jornada" route of the Santa Fe Trail.

Wade Gaddis was a farmer. In 1922 he sold their farm to move his family to Haviland so his children could enjoy a Christian education.

Haviland is located in Kiowa County, 100 miles due west of Wichita on old U.S. Route 54. Population: 700.

Located in the vicinity of the world-famous Haviland Meteor Crater, it is named for Laura Smith Haviland (1808-1898), a Canadian-born Quaker and abolitionist who played a prominent role in the organization and operation of the Underground Railroad. Beginning in the 1830s, the Havilands were the first in Michigan to shelter fugitive slaves from the South on their way to freedom in Canada.

By 1931, Eli was principal of Friends Bible College, the former Haviland Academy, now Barclay College. Alice was an alumna of the school, class of 1929.

After graduation, she trained as a nurse in Newton, Kan. Returning to Kiowa County to teach in a rural school, she married Eli on April 16, 1931.

Until the 1940s, the Wheelers had done pastoral work with Friends churches in New Providence (Iowa), Kansas City and Los Angeles.

In 1945 they left for Africa, to Kivimba, northeast of Lake Tanganyika, in what is today the Republic of Burundi.

While he worked securing permits to operate a hospital and school, Alice initiated an early childhood education program and assisted in irrigating hillside farming plots.

Together, they helped form a leper colony, presided over a missions organization, and spoke at numerous conferences.

With Eli gone, Alice returned to the states, along with son Ned and daughter Eletta. She became a registered nurse by attending classes in both Emporia, Kan., and Phoenix, Ariz.

Moving to Newberg so her children could attend George Fox College (both did and both graduated), Alice found "full-time" employment by working three jobs: as a residence hall director, as a campus nurse, and as a staff nurse at Newberg Community Hospital, now Providence Newberg Hospital.

Then something extraordinary happened.

Local churches and GFC students raised enough money to send her back to Africa to complete the work at the leper colony she and husband Eli had helped start.

According to her obituary in the June 6, 1998, *Newberg Graphic*, "Her decision to return insured the survival of the facility, which had been threatened with closure due to a lack of medical personnel."

Aside from Alice's story, but soon to be related, in 1954 George Fox appointed Milo Ross as its eighth president. He had just lost his wife, Helen, to chronic illness. A recent arrival to Oregon himself, he had first served the college as a part-time student recruiter.

On Oct. 10, 1955, Milo married Alice. The couple remained inseparable until his death in 1979.

Under their guidance, the school liquidated its debt, gained full accreditation with the Northwest Association of Secondary and Higher Schools, doubled the college's enrollment, built six new buildings, and renovated and remodeled eight others.

In the 1960s, the two traveled on goodwill missions for the school to 24 countries, while also helping to conduct summer programs in the Middle East. After his retirement in 1969, Milo became president of the George Fox Foundation and stayed in the position until his passing.

As a part of her efforts to help her president/husband navigate GFC through the financially lean years of the 1950s, Alice would often forgo her salary to make sure the college's payroll was met.

One year prior to Milo's death, the couple saw the opening of George Fox University's Ross Center, home now to the departments of the visual and performing arts.

It includes the Bauman Auditorium, Lindgren Gallery, two rehearsal halls, 16 practice rooms and several classrooms. The organ housed in Bauman was a gift of the Rosses.

On May 30, 1998, this former George Fox "first lady" died at Friendsview Manor here in Newberg. She was 87.

Alice's passing came nine days after the loss of former George Fox president Edward F. Stevens (president from 1983-1997) to a brain tumor. ❖

In the days of "auto neon"

According to a Google search, neon was discovered in 1898 by two Londoners, Sir William Ramsay and Morris Travers.

By 1910, neon had advanced to the point where Air Liquide co-founder Georges Claude could demonstrate modern neon lighting using a sealed tube. By 1912 Claude was selling his tubes as advertising signs.

The first appearance of the new lighting in the U.S. came in the 1920s. The place was a Packard auto dealership in Los Angeles.

Unfortunately, Google was a bit fuzzy about how neon lighting made its way to the roof of the pizza delivery car.

However, when someone does get around to documenting the progression, Newberg may have a contribution make.

Welcome to the story of local inventor Walter J. Pawelski.

In 1952, Pawelski, service manager of Butler Chevrolet's garage on E. First, began work on an idea for a neon sign for his truck.

As we've seen, the neon part had already been worked out. Still unsolved was how to power the light riding atop a motor vehicle.

By December, Pawelski had developed a device connecting his truck battery to his sign in a way that wouldn't drain the battery. If this doesn't sound like much, in the early 1950s it was a big deal.

Companies like General Motors had been working on car neon for several years, but GM's sign required 35 amperes of current, far too much for batteries of the time.

By 1954, Pawelski's battery could light 30-feet of neon tubing with one ampere of current. By comparison, car headlights in the 1950s used eight amperes.

In early trials, he had operated his sign for three continuous days without his battery working up a sweat.

By March 1954 (2014 is the 60th anniversary), Pawelski was ready to go into production.

First he rented a Quonset hut on North Blaine. Next he hired three men to do the work.

Longtime residents of the city remember this location well because it once housed two Quonset huts, one of which was used by Ken and Joan Austin in 1965 to relocate their (at that time) nascent A-dec dental manufacturing company from Colorado to Newberg.

The A-dec Quonset is a museum on the company's campus. The second one is still there, 109 N. Blaine, and has housed a number of businesses over the years.

I haven't been able to find out which one Pawelski used.

Pawelski named his company Auto Neon. His wife, Charlotte, served as manager while he continued in his position at Butler.

In an interview with the *Graphic* for the March 25, 1954, edition, Pawelski said he had turned down numerous offers to buy his invention, preferring to market the product himself.

He added he already had enough contracts in hand to anticipate he would soon need six employees.

At the time the article appeared, a patent had been applied for and the name of the company had been recorded with the state.

To the skeptics who told him the neon tubing would not stand up to the vibrations of moving motor vehicle, he explained that if adjusted loosely, the sign and tubing would hold up without any problems.

When asked by the newspaper what might be the uses of his new invention, Pawelski delivered one for the ages:

"Bread companies," he responded, "and cleaners and florists, and other firms using panel trucks. Also, garages, service stations, wrecking car firms and many other companies."

But no pizza.

A photo on the front page of the newspaper that day showed Pawelski's Chevy pickup with his first neon sign sitting proudly on top.

It read, "Butler Chev Co". ❖

SOURCES
AND INDEX

SOURCES

This list is intended to be both a record of the books, articles, documents and websites used to write this book, as well as a guide to anyone wanting to know more about the history of Newberg, the ancient geology of the area and the Native American culture that thrived here long before the arrival of the pioneers.

A Century to Remember: Newberg 1889-1989. Special commemorative tabloid published by the *Newberg Graphic* in February 1989. Hereafter cited as *CTR*.

A Photographic History of Yamhill County. Vancouver, Wash.: Pediment Publishing, 2002.

Allen, John Eliot; Marjorie Burns; and Sam C. Sargent. *Cataclysms on the Columbia*. Portland: Timber Press, 1986. Ancient geology of Willamette Valley.

Allen. "Catastrophic Floods Sculpted Newberg Landscape." Frederickson, Keith (ed.). *CTR*, Feb. 22, 1989, pp. 6-7.

Baseball-Almanac.com (Statistics about the baseball careers of Billy Sullivan and Fielder Jones). Sullivan and Jones were teammates on the 1906 Chicago White Sox baseball team, which won the World Series that year and which is known to baseball historians as the "Hitless Wonders." Sullivan retired to grow filberts on a farm west of Newberg. Jones was his partner in the venture, was a successful Portland businessman, and served as head baseball coach at Oregon Agricultural College in 1910.

BaseballLibrary.com (Billy Sullivan and Fielder Jones).

Beckham, Stephen Dow. *The Indians of Western Oregon: This Land was Theirs*. Coos Bay: Arago Books, 1977.

Beebe, Ralph K. *A Heritage to Honor, a Future to Fulfill: George Fox College 1891-1991*. Newberg: The Barclay Press, 1991. Excellent research and writing. Contains a lot of history of Newberg not found anywhere else.

Beebe. *The Garden of the Lord*. Newberg: The Barclay Press, 1968.

"Billy Sullivan Dies in Newberg at 89." *The Newberg Graphic*, published at end of January or early February, 1965. Hereafter cited as *Graphic*.

Blodgett, Robert B. and McCracken, T. *Holy Roller: Murder and Madness in Oregon's Love Cult*. Caldwell, Idaho: Caxton Press, 2002. This book has considerable information regarding Newberg resident George Mitchell, who played a significant role in this amazing story of one of Oregon's most infamous religious cults.

Bretz, J. Harlen. "The Channeled Scabland of the Columbia Plateau." *Journal of Geology*, Vol. 31, 1923, pp. 617-649.

Bretz. "The Spokane flood beyond the Channeled Scablands." *Journal of Geology*, Vol. 33, 1925, pp. 97-115, 236-259.

Bretz; Smith, H.T.U.; and Neff, G.E. "Channeled Scabland of Washington—New Data and Interpretations." *Geological Society of America Bulletin*, Vol. 67, 1956, pp. 957-1049.

SOURCES

Buan, Carolyn M. and Richard Lewis (ed.). *The First Oregonians*. Portland: Oregon Council for the Humanities, 1991.

Burden, Amanda. "Unique home may soon receive its due." *Graphic*, Sept. 12, 1998, p. 1. Contains history of Paulson-Gregory House, 509 S. College. Listed on National Register of Historic Places.

Burner, David. *Herbert Hoover: A Public Life*. New York: Alfred A. Knopf, 1979, pp. 1-43.

Cadd, Dick. *Four Flats and a Pitchpipe*. Published by the author: Newberg, OR, 2003. An excellent history of one of Newberg's most famous singing groups.

Cady, King and Dimond, Chester A. (pub.). *Newberg Graphic 50th Anniversary Progress Edition*, April 1939.

"Celebrate Camellia Day: Newberg will recognize city flower next month." *Graphic*, March 25, 2009, p. 1.

City of Newberg. *Index of Historic Properties*, 1985. On file at the Newberg Public Library and the Yamhill County Historical Society

"Cooking up Camas (camassia quamash)." *Historic Marion*, Vol. 30, No. 4, May 1992, p. 4. History of Native Americans in the Willamette Valley and Yamhill County.

Cooper, J.C. *Military History of Yamhill County: 1899*. No publisher or date of publication given. Copy on file at Newberg Public Library. The author says that U.S. Navy Commodore Charles Wilkes, on a visit to the Willamette Valley in 1841, referred to the northern parts of Polk and Yamhill counties as the "Faulitz Valley."

Corning, Howard McKinley. *Willamette Landings: Ghost Towns of the River*. Portland: Oregon Historical Society, 1947.

"Death of Pioneer of Chehalem Valley." *Graphic*, Oct. 10, 1918, p. 1

Dent, Paul and McCain, Robert (pub.). *Newberg Graphic: Diamond Anniversary* (edition), 1964.

Dobbs, Caroline C. *The Men of Champoeg*. Metropoltan (sic) Press, Portland, Oregon, 1932. Reprinted in 1993 by the Oregon Society of The National Society of the Daughters of the American Revolution.

Edmonston, George P. Jr., "Tales from the Grubby End." Newberg history column in the *Graphic*, March 2011-present. The Newberg Public Library keeps manuscript copy of the series in a three-ring binder found in the Newberg history section.

Edmonston. "Fielder Jones." *The Oregon Stater*. Corvallis: Oregon State University Alumni Association, Oct. 1998, p. 28.

Edmonston. "George Mitchell and the Holy Rollers." *The Oregon Stater*. Corvallis: Oregon State University Alumni Association, Dec. 1995, p. 32.

SOURCES

Edmonston. "Fiery story lies beneath cold grave." *Newberg Graphic*, Feb. 1, 1995. The story of Oregon's Creffield Cult and Newberg's connection to it.

Edmonston. *All I Wanted Was an Opportunity: The Story of George Kenneth Austin Jr.* Unpublished manuscript in possession of Mr. Austin and Austin family. The most comprehensive history of the A-dec dental company yet produced. Includes information on the life and contributions of Joan Austin.

Edwards, C.J. "Newberg As It Was Fifty Years Ago." *Newberg Graphic 50ᵗʰ Anniversary Progress Edition*, April 1939.

Edwards, Jesse. Biography found in *Portrait and Biographical Record of the Willamette Valley, Oregon*. Chicago: Chapman Publishing Co., 1903, pp. 303-304.

Edwards, Lowell and Edwards, Margaret. *Miles Lowell Edwards: His Ancestors and Descendants*. Santa Ana, Calif.: Pioneer Press, 1972, pp. 29-49.

Etulain, Richard W. *Beyond the Missouri: The Story of the American West*. Albuquerque: The University of New Mexico Press, 2006, pp. 6-37.Everest, Granville. "Early Newberg Band History Told by Pioneer." *Newberg Scribe*, March 17, 1932.

Fitzgibbon, Joe. "A Life at the Movies." *The Oregonian*, Jan.1, 1998.

Frederickson (ed.). "The Graphic: A Century of News." *CTR*, Feb. 22, 1989, pp. 55-57.

Frederickson, Keith (ed.). *CTR,* Feb. 22, 1989.

Friedman, Ralph. *In Search of Western Oregon*. Caldwell, Idaho: The Claxton Press, 1990.

Fuller, Tom and Van Heukelem, Christy. *Images of America: Newberg*. Arcadia Publishing, 2010. The largest collection of vintage Newberg photos in one publication available at present, most from the archives of the Yamhill County Historical Society and George Fox University.

Gatschet, Albert Samuel. *The Klamath Indians of Southwestern Oregon* is a classic in the study of the Native Americans in Oregon. Gatschet (1832-1907) was a pioneer in the study of Native American Languages who worked for the U.S. Geological Society and became a member of the Bureau of American Ethnology.

Genealogical Forum of Portland (pub.). *Records of Provisional Land Claims: 1845-1849*. Detailed accounts of the earliest settlers of Yamhill County.

Genealogical Forum of Portland (pub.). *Oregon Donation Land Claims: 1850-1855*.

Graphic. Diamond Anniversary Edition, 1964.

Graphic. Oregon Centennial Edition, May 14, 1959.

For information about Newberg's first settlers see: *Graphic*, Jan. 12, 1889, p. 2; *Graphic*, Jan 19, 1889, p. 2; *Graphic*, Jan. 26, 1889, p. 2; *Graphic*, Feb. 2, 1889, p. 2; *Graphic*, Feb. 16, 1889, p. 2; *Graphic*, Feb. 23, 1889, p. 2; "Prof. Macy On Early History." *Graphic*, Dec.12, 1929, p.1, 12.

SOURCES

Hadley, William Macy. "Correspondence of William Macy Hadley, May to November, 1875." Folder located in Northwest Yearly Meeting, Archives, George Fox University.

Haight, Abby. "Drive-In's owner puts passion into big screen." *The Oregonian: Southwest Weekly.* May 29, 2008, pp. 6-7.

Helm, Mike (ed.). *The Lockley Files: Conversations with Pioneer Women.* Eugene, Oregon: Rainy Day Press, 1993, pp. 165-169.

Helm. *The Lockley Files: Conversations with Pioneer Men.* Eugene, Oregon: Rainy Day Press, 1996, pp. 94-96.

The later writings of Alexander Henry the Younger, written before his death in Astoria by drowning in 1814, have eyewitness accounts from this explorer of the Yamhelas, one of a number of Indian bands living in the Newberg area and throughout western Oregon, collectively known as the Kalapuyas. The date and place of Henry's birth are not known. His journal of 1799–1814, edited by Elliott Coues (together with the journal of David Thompson) as *New Light on the Early History of the Greater Northwest* (1897), describes his adventures as a trader of the North West Company on the Red, Pembina, Saskatchewan, and Columbia rivers and is particularly valuable for its account of the native tribes of these regions.

Hill, Joseph J. "Ewing Young in the Fur Trade of the Far Southwest, 1822-1834." *Oregon Historical Quarterly,* March 1923. *Hereafter cited as OHQ.*

Hobson, Jessie. "Looking Backward." *Graphic,* Nov. 14, 1912.

Hobson, William. Letter to Elam Jessup, brother-in-law, dated July 4, 1877. Photocopy courtesy Dr. Robert Holveck, DVM, Newberg.

Hobson. Letter to Elam Jessup, Jan. 23, 1886. Photocopy courtesy Newberg veterinarian Dr. Robert Holveck.

Holmes, Kenneth L. *Ewing Young: Master Trapper.* Portland: Binford & Mort, Publishers, 1967.

Photo of Hoover-Minthorn home before Bert Brown Barker remodel found in *Newberg Graphic,* June 18, 1986. Article is titled "A Walk Through History."

Hoover, Herbert: *Presidential Library & Museum* website.

Hoover, Herbert. *The Memoirs of Herbert Hoover: Years of Adventure: 1874-1920.* New York: The Macmillan Company, 1951, pp. 1-24.

"House on the corner returns to George Fox." *Graphic,* Nov. 27, 1993. Story of the Levi Pennington house at 1000 Sheridan St. built in 1904.

Huffman, Doris A. Jones. *The Everests: A Family History of Yamhill County.* Unpublished manuscript, 1999 copyright held by daughter Corinne A. Waterbury, Seattle, Washington. Written prior to Ms. Huffman's death in 1997 and edited by the Oregon Historical Society.

Huffman. *The Everests,* pp. 121-122.

Huffman. "He Fashioned Shoes for Horses--and Humans." *CTR*, p. 27.

Huffman. "Hess Built Gristmill on Chehalem Creek." *CTR*, p. 26.

Huffman. "Homesteading Chehalem's 'Grubby End.' " *CTR*, p. 25.

Huffman. "Newberg's Name has Roots in Bavaria." *CTR*, p. 29.

Huffman. "Ramsey Sawmill Helped Build Newberg." *CTR*, p. 15.

Huffman. "A Splendid Life Lived to the Fullest." *CTR*, p. 28.

Huffman. "A Tale of Gold, Saloons and Race Horses." *CTR*, p. 24.

Humphrey, Tom. "Profile of Newberg," Parts 1-5. *Oregon Journal*. Nov. 26-30, 1956.

Hussey, John A. *Champoeg: A Place of Transition*. Portland: Oregon Historical Society, et. al., 1967.

Irwin, Will. *Herbert Hoover: A Reminiscent Biography*. New York and London: The Century Company, 1928, pp. 3-68.

"James Lewelling, Last Member of Lincoln Body Guard, Died Wednesday, Aged 94." *Graphic*, March 7, 1935. James' family also had connections to the import to Oregon of the Bing cherry.

Johnson, Craig. "History docks at Rogers Landing." *Graphic*, Sept. 28, 1988, p. 7.

Johnson, Oscar. "The Kalapuya."*Clackamas County History*, Spring 1999.

Jones Hall: "Early Hall Being Razed: Newberg Losing Old Landmark." *The Oregonian*, March 26, 1940. Writer says this was Newberg's first town hall, located at the corner of First and Main. Built in 1888.

Kadel, Steve. "On with the show." *The Oregonian*, June 1992.

Kallas, John. "Wapato: Indian Potato." *Wilderness Way*, Vol. 9, Issue 1, 2004.

Kidd, Ed. "Chance Visit Drew Quakers to Newberg." *CTR*, p. 49.

Kidd. "Ewing Young and the Birth of a Territory." *CTR*, p. 14.

Kidd. "Quaker School an Integral Part of Newberg." *CTR*, pp. 50-53.

Lomax, Alfred L. "Union Woolen Mill Company: *Newberg Enterprise*, Various issues, 1910-1912.

Lyons, Eugene. *Herbert Hoover: A Biography*. New York: Doubleday and Company, 1964, pp. 1-35.

MacGregor, John. *The Progress of America from the Discovery of America to the Year 1846*. London: Whittaker Co., 1847, p. 490, in which MacGregor says Capt. (Commodore) Wilkes "crossed the Yam Hills to the Faulitz plains."

Mackey, Harold. *The Kalapuyans: A Sourcebook on the Indians of the Willamette Valley*. Salem: Mission Mill Museum Association, 1974.

SOURCES

Macy, Perry D. "Early Days in Newberg Vicinity." *Graphic*, April 1939. A professor of history at Pacific College, Mr. Macy was a well-known local historian who interviewed many old timers around Newberg.

Malinowski, Sharon and Anna Sheets(eds.). *The Gale Encyclopedia of Native American Tribes*. Detroit, MI: Thomas Gale Publishing , Vol. 4, 1998, pp. 344-348.

Maps produced by the Sanborn-Perris Map and Publishing Company, Broadway Avenue, New York, N.Y. Found in Newberg Public Library for years 1891, 1892, 1902, 1905, 1912 and 1929.

McArthur, Lewis A. and McArthur, Lewis L. *Oregon Geographic Names*. Portland: Oregon Historical Society Press. Sixth Edition, 1992.

McCain, Bob. "Graphic's centennial coming up." *Graphic,* June 8, 1988, pp. 11, 13.

McKay, Harvey J. *St. Paul, Oregon: 1830-1890*. Portland: Binford & Mort, 1980.

McNicols, Donald. *Portrait of a Quaker: Levi T. Pennington (1875-1975), A Critical Biography*. Newberg: The Barclay Press, 1980.

Metsker, Charles F. *Metsker's Atlas of Yamhill County, Oregon*. May, 1942, p. 4. This page has map of all original DLC's in Newberg.

Miller, Jennie D. *A History of Newberg: 1936-1937-1938*. Unpublished manuscript in possession of author. Copy also on file at Newberg Public Library. Covers considerably more than years listed in title and a treasure of a resource for anyone wanting to know about the history of Newberg up to 1940.

Miller. "Pacific College and Academy." *A History of Newberg*, pp. 68-70. Valuable for understanding the early history of George Fox University.

Miller. "Newspapers." *A History of Newberg*, p. 67.

"Miller Mercantile Direct Descendant of First General Merchandise Store in City." *Graphic*, March 21, 1935, p. 1. Gives location of Newberg's first store based on the recollections of the city's oldest residents.

Motor boat races on the Willamette River in 1921. *Graphic*, May 14, 2014.

Nedry, H.S. "Willamette Valley in 1859: Diary of a Tour." *OHQ*, Vol. 46, No. 3, September 1945, pp. 235-254.

Nedry. "The Friends Come to Oregon." *OHQ*, Vol. 45, September 1944, pp. 196-197.

"Newberg at the turn of the century." *McMinnville News-Register*. Featured in the "Time Machine" series. Photo only. Image taken sometime between 1905-1909.

Newman, Amanda. "WWII life floats manufactured in Newberg." *Graphic*, Oct. 27, 2007.

"One of Oregon's Historic Spots to be Marked Soon." *Newberg Scribe*, Feb. 4, 1932.

SOURCES

O'Neil, Shirley H. *Yamhill County Pioneers*. Vols. I and II. Self-published, 2004. Detailed information about Yamhill County's earliest settlers.

O'Neil. *Yamhill County Pioneers: Study of the Inhabitants Listed in the 1850 Federal Census for Yamhill County, Oregon, Volume II*. Self-published, 2004. For information regarding Newberg's earliest Quaker settlers setting up land claims between Newberg and Dundee, see p. 510. See also Lockett, Jim and Reita, "Tales of the Trail," *McMinnville News-Register*, Nov. 20, 1993.

Oregon History Project online: "Faulitz River from Yam Hills." Joseph Drayton, a member of the U.S. Exploring Expedition that explored the Pacific Rim from 1838-1842 made sketches of a trip to the north Willamette Valley in which he refers to the Yamhill River as the Faulitz River.

"Outlook for 1932 Varied on Farms." *Newberg Scribe*, March 17, 1932.

"Pacific Academy, Faculty and Student Body: 1885-86." *Graphic*, Aug. 30, 1917, p. 1.

Perisho, Stephen Z. *A History of the Newberg Monthly Meeting, 1878-1893*. Senior research paper and unpublished manuscript located in the Murdock Learning Resource Center, George Fox University Library. Dated June 13, 1983.

Perisho. *A History of the Newberg Monthly Meeting*, pp. 41-46.

Perisho. *A History of the Newberg Monthly Meeting*, pp. 29-32.

Philbrick, Nathaniel. *Sea of Glory: America's Voyage of Discovery, the U.S. Exploring Expedition, 1838-1842*. Viking, 2003.

Pioneer Families of Yamhill County: Biographical Sketches of Persons Listed in the U.S. Government Census of 1850. Copy in the Newberg Public Library. Probably the best written source available for Newberg's first settlers.

Post Office: For information on early postal service to Newberg see Miller, *History of Newberg*, p. 71; *Graphic*. "Sam Parrett Tells City History," Dec. 9, 1943; *Oregon Geographical Names*, pp. 170, 563, 617, and 893.

Rees, John Howard. *Memoirs of John Howard Rees*. Northwest Yearly Meeting Archives, George Fox University.

Red Electric train history found at *PdxHistory.com*

Reddy, John. "Three churches, 10 decades: Newberg parish marks 100 years." *Catholic Sentinel*, Vol. 138, No. 37, Sept. 14, 2007, pp. 1, 10-12.

"Remember the Wet-Dry Wars?" *Graphic*, CTR, pp. 108-109. How Newberg legalized the sale of alcohol.

Robbins, William G. "Surviving the Great Depression: The New Deal in Oregon." *OHQ*, Vol. 109, No. 2, Summer 2008, pp. 311-317.

Rojas-Burke, Joe. "Mechanical heart valve still ticking." *The Oregonian*, May 28, 2008, p. B5.

SOURCES

Ross, Alexander. *Adventures of the first settlers on the Oregon or Columbia River: Being a narrative of the expedition fitted out by John Jacob Astor to establish the Pacific Fur Company with an account of some Indian tribes of the coast of the Pacific.* London: Smith, Elder and Co., 1849. Reprinted as Ross, Alexander. *Adventures of the First Settlers on the Oregon or Columbia River, 1810-1813.* Lincoln: University of Nebraska Press, 1986.

"Safe Wreckers Visit Newberg." *Graphic*, Oct. 23, 1908. The story was reprinted in the *Graphic* on Nov. 13, 1969, p. 3.

Sale, David. "Local officials return to Chehalem Strategic Plan," *Graphic*, Oct. 1, 2008, p. A6.

Sale. "Library will celebrate the past, look to the future." *Graphic*, May 28, 2008.

Sale. "Hazelden will break ground on $10 million expansion." *Graphic*, Oct. 8, 2008, p. A11.

"Sam Parrish Tells City History." *Graphic*, Dec. 9, 1943, p. 1.

Schomburg, Alex. See Steve Duin's feature story about the world-famous comic book illustrator in *Oregon Northwest* magazine, March 24, 1991.

Schwantes, Carlos. *The Pacific Northwest: An Interpretive History.* Lincoln: The University of Nebraska Press, 1989.

Scott, Leslie M. "Soil Repairs in Willamette Valley." *OHQ*, Vol. 28, No. 1 March 1917, pp. 54-68.

Scott. "History of the Narrow Gauge Railroad in the Willamette Valley." *OHQ*, Vo. XX, No. 2, June 1919.

Scotty, Christie. "Pursuing Their Own Agenda." *Graphic*, Jan. 1, 2003.

Scotty, Christie and Trampush, Amy. "The memory of a baseball." *Graphic*. Sept. 5, 2001.

Shinn, Paul. "Eugene in the Depression: 1929-1935." *OHQ*, Vol. 86, No. 4, pp. 341-370.

Smith, John E. *Corvallis College.* Self-published, 1953, p. 19. Mr. Smith was a founding member of the Benton County Historical Society and copies of this small booklet, printed in Corvallis, are rare.

"Some Old Landmarks: How They Have Shifted From Time to Time To Meet New Conditions." *Graphic*, Jan. 20, 1910, p.1.

Souvenir Edition of the Newberg Graphic, 1805-1905: Centennial of Old Oregon, July 13, 1905.

Stark, Peter. *Astoria: Astor and Jefferson's Lost Pacific Empire.* Ecco Press/Harper Collins, 2014.

Stoller, Ruth. *Old Yamhill. The Early History of Its Towns and Cities.* Portland: Binford & Mort Publishers, 1976. Hereafter cited as *Old Yamhill.* Stoller remains a legend among local historians and genealogists and was a founding member of the YCHS.

Stoller. "Newberg: Two Towns in One." *Old Yamhill, 1976,* pp. 59-63. The best article yet written on early Newberg.

Stoller. (ed.). *Schools of Old Yamhill.* Lafayette: Yamhill County Historical Society, 1982, pp. vi-vii, 4, 42-43.

Students of Newberg public schools, grades 6-8, 1905. Written assignments prepared for the Lewis and Clark Exposition covering the topics of Newberg business and industry and well-known local landmarks, assembled and bound together by teachers, Etta McCoy, Evangeline Martin, and F.H. Buchanan. Housed in Newberg Public Library vertical files, Newberg History. Contains descriptions not found anywhere else and extremely rare original photos of interiors and exteriors of businesses and their owners.

"Successful Decade." *OHQ,* June 1952, No. 2. p. 100.

Takeda, Chijo. "Stones with history." *Graphic,* Sept. 5, 1998. Short feature about Friends Cemetery. Nice photos.

Terry, John. "An ache for acreage entitled homesteaders to title, lands." *The Oregonian,* Feb.15, 1998.

Terry. "Settler's claim frames fuzzy state of land laws, justice." *The Sunday Oregonian,* Dec. 4, 2005.

Touring Newberg old homes and neighborhoods: "A Walk Through History." *Graphic,* Oct. 16, 1991. See also: *Historic Newberg: A Walking Tour of the Northside Neighborhood.* Pamphlet written and published by the Newberg Old Fashioned Festival Walking Tour Committee. Issue year and date unknown but probably mid-1990s. An additional source is through the Newberg Downtown Coalition's website and its excellent links to history features on the Newberg business district.

"Van Valins Killed." *Graphic,* Nov. 3, 1955. Prominent Newberg dentist and wife killed in tragic plane crash outside Denver in 1955. See also *Life Magazine,* Vol. 39, No. 22, Nov. 28, 1955.

Van Valin, Minnie. *Pioneer Families of Yamhill County.*

"VFW history in Newberg." George L. Wright Newberg Post 4015. Manuscript copy held by post and in personal collection of George Edmonston Jr.

"Voice of Experience Dies." *Graphic,* Feb. 5, 1942, p. 1. Source for life of Marion S. Taylor and his connection to Newberg. Marion Taylor obit on file at YCHS. Unidentified newspaper article, probably from McMinnville newspaper.

Walters, Betty Lawson. "The Lean Years: John L. Casteel's Diaries, 1931-42." *OHQ,* Vol. 89, No. 1, pp. 229-301.

Wert, Hal Elliott. *Hoover: The Fishing President. Portrait of the Private Man and His Life Outdoors.* Mechanicsburg, Penn.: Stackpole Books, 2005, pp. 21-39.

SOURCES

"White Sox Orchard." *Graphic*, May 2, 1912, p. 1.

Wiley, Dennis. "Kalapuya: A Culture in Harmony with the Earth." *CTR*, p. 11.

Wiley. "Champoeg: A Storehouse of Treasures." *CTR*, p. 10.

"Will Close for Afternoon Chautauqua Programs." *Graphic*, July 5, 1917, p.1. (Story includes a list of downtown businesses.)

Wilmot, Mrs. Frank: *Oregon Boys at War: Letters from Oregon Boys in France, Second Book*. Portland: Glass & Prudhomme Company, 1918.

Woodward, E.H. "Business interests of Newberg and Vicinity." *Graphic*, Feb. 6, 1903. Includes brief descriptions of F.A. Morris, Newberg Land Company; A.B. Cooper Meat Market; H.J. Austin Meat Market; Newberg Commercial Stables; Newberg Creamery; T.B. Cummings Furniture and Undertaking; C.B. Wilson, Groceryman; C.F. Moore, Druggist; Bank of Newberg; Chehalem Valley Mills; Pinney Lumber Yard, and more.

Woodward. "Business interests of Newberg and vicinity." *Graphic*, Feb. 13, 1903. Includes Hollingsworth and Cooper, furniture and undertaking, E. 1st Street. Paper shows evidence that some Newberg merchants and shoppers were still using gold coins.

Woodward. "What of the Future?" *Newberg Graphic*, Nov. 26, 1908.

Woodward, E.H. (Mrs.). "Early Days of the Quakers in Newberg." *Newberg Graphic, 50th Anniversary Edition*. April 1939

Work, John. "John Work's Journey from Fort Vancouver to Umpqua River, and Return, in 1834. Introduction and comments by Leslie M. Scott. *OHQ*, Vol. 24, No. 3, Sept. 1923, pp. 238-268.

World War I. "Former Newberg Boy Killed in France." *Graphic*, Oct. 10, 1918, p.1.

World War I: Letters from Europe written by Newberg locals serving war. *Graphic*, April 1917 through Dec. 1918.

Youngberg, Elsie. *Oregon Territory: 1850 Census*. Lebanon, Oregon: End of the Trail Publishers, 1970, pp. 277-310. Census figures show there were 243 families living in the Newberg area by 1850.

Young, F.G. "Ewing Young and His Estate." *OHQ*, September 1920.

Young, F. Harold (ed.). "William Hobson, Quaker Missionary." *OHQ*, June, 1933, pp. 134-143. Includes passages from Hobson's diary.

Zenk, Henry B. "Kalapuyans." *Handbook of North American Indians*. Washington, D.C.: Smithsonian Institution, Vol. 7, 1990, pp. 547-553.

INDEX

INDEX

E

Earlham College, 50
Edwards, Clarence, 44-45
Edwards, Jesse, 40-44
Edwards, Margaret, 47
Edwards, Mabel, 40
Edwards, Mary Kemp, 40
Edwards Miles Lowell, 44-47
Edwards, O.K., 40
Emery, Orm C., 101
Evening Star, 100
Everest, Richard, 30
Everest, Jane, 30

F

Farmeroo, 107
Farm Product Show, 107
Felton, Rob, 114
Fendall, Amanda, 30
Fendall, Charles, 30
Foster, Richard James, 129
Francis, Ted, 103
Frederick, William Jr., 127
French Prairie, 22
Friends Pacific Academy, 39
Friendsview Manor, 103
Frink, Elsie, see Elsie Leavitt
Foster, Richard James, 129
Four Flats, 129

G

Gainer, Russel, 103
GAR, see Grand Army of the Republic
Garrard, Lewis, 23
Gay, George, 26
Gervais, Jean Baptiste, 23
Gervais, Joseph, 23
Giebenhain, Todd, 129
"Goat Woman", see Elizabeth McBroom
Goat Lady, see Elizabeth McBroom
Graham, Bertha, 137
Grand Army of the Republic, 59
Gravel, Gideon, 29
Graves, Alvin T., 64
Graves, G.A., 101

Great Depression, 98-99
Griffith, Leah, 8
"Grubby End", **throughout**

H

Hagie, Levi, (also Hagey), 30
"Hamburger Gladys", see Gladys Auld
Harper, Bob, 101
Harris, Moses "Black", 23
Haworth, John, 69
Hembree, Absalom J., 33-34
Hembree, Nancy, 33
Hess Creek, 15
Hess, Joseph, 29, 40
Hess, Mary, 29
Highway 99W, 94-95
Hobson, William, 37, 38, 43
Hotel Purdy, 86
Hubbel, Mrs. O.V., 103
Honey Creek Friends Meeting, 39
Hoover, Herbert, 10, 51-53, 142-143
Hopkins, Henry, 59
Huffman, Doris, 12
Hutchens, Elijah, 40
Hutchins, R.N., 72

I

"I-5 Killer," see David Bishop
Inglis, Margaret, 105
Iverson, Melvin S., 64

J

Jensen, Charles W., 64
Johnson, Edward H., 77
Jones, Fielder, 120, 123-124

K

Kamph, Michael C., 77Kanyon Hall, see Minthorn Hall
Keller, William, 69
Kenworth, Melvin, 76
Kidd, Florence Rebecca, see Rebecca Pennington
Ku Klux Klan, 117-119

161

INDEX

INDEX

United Airlines Flight 629, 115-116

V

Vancouver, Fort, 22
Vanderbeck, Herman, 64
Van Valin, Minnie, 13, 115-116
Van Valin, Ralph, 115-116
Vinson, Isaac, 91
"Voice of Experience," see Marion Sale Taylor
Volstead Act, 111

W

Walker, Oliver J., 38
Wallace, William, 29
Warren, Perry, 110
Waters, Bertha May, 50
Wedin, Clara, 134
Welch, Amelia, 30
Welch, John, 30
West Coast Telephone Company, 98
"Wet-Dry Wars", 110-111
Wheeler, Alice G., see Alice Ross
Wheeler, Eli, 145
Wilhite, Steve, 56
White Sox Orchard, 123-124
Whitmore, Lloyd, 64

Whitney, Dick, 77-78
Whittier Literary Society, 104
Willamette Post, 15, 17
Williamson, John, 30
Williamson, Susan, 30
Women's Christian Temperance Movement, 110
Women's Temperance League, 104
Wood, David, 38, 40
Wood, Maggie, 40
Woodman, Don, 101
Wood-Mar Hall, 48-49, 106
Woods, Joe, 90
Woodward, Amanda, 40, 48-49
Woodward, Ezra H., 9, 40, 97, 101
Woodward, Walter C., 40
Wright, George L., 69-71

Y

Yakima War, 33
Yamhill Independent, The, 101
Young, Ewing, 23, 25-27
Youngs, Richard P., 64

Z

Zielaskowski, Alfred M., 68

George P. Edmonston Jr.

George P. Edmonston Jr. is a native of Baton Rouge, Louisiana. He attended high school in Ocean Springs, Mississippi, then earned a bachelor's degree in history from Louisiana State University in 1971 and master's degree in history from the University of Louisiana-Lafayette in 1974. At LSU, George studied with Pulitzer Prize-winning historian, T. Harry Williams.

In 1983 George became the founding editor of *LSU Magazine* at his alma mater.

Relocating to Oregon and the Pacific Northwest in 1986, he served for 20 years as editor of Oregon State University's alumni magazine, *The Oregon Stater*. During this time he did extensive work researching and writing about the history of OSU, its alumni and athletic programs.

Under his leadership, the publication won 16 regional and national awards from the Council for the Advancement of Education in Washington, D.C. At the university, George held faculty rank and was president of the Student Media Advisory Committee from 2004-2006.

After his retirement in 2005, George enjoyed a six-year period (2006-2011) as the Oregon Stater's history and traditions editor. He also conducted history tours of the OSU campus at homecoming and class reunions for visiting alumni.

In 2003 he co-authored the book Tales from Oregon State Sports.

He has published over 180 articles on Oregon and OSU history in the *Cultural Heritage Courier,* the *Albany Democrat-Herald,* the *Corvallis Gazette-Times,* the *Newberg Graphic, The Oregonian,* and the *Salem Statesman-Journal.* Since March 2011, he has enjoyed a position as columnist with the *Graphic,* where his "Tales from the Grubby End" appears twice monthly.

In 2004 George was selected by Ken and Joan Austin, co-founders and co-owners of A-dec, Inc., the world's leading manufacturer of dental equipment, to serve as their family historian. He stayed in this capacity for six years, during which time he authored a biography of Ken and also completed a 132-page historical timeline for A-dec.

George has provided two entries for *The Oregon Encyclopedia,* the first concerning the life of basketball star Wade "Swede" Halbrook, the second a company profile of A-dec.

In August 2010 he co-founded (with his wife, Lucy) the Newberg Historical Society and served as its president for two years.

In 2007 George became the recipient of the OSU Alumni Association's Honorary Alumni Award, which gives official alumni status to someone who does not hold a degree from the university. In the 139-year history of the Association, only seven individuals have been honored with this award.

George is a past member of the board of trustees of the Benton County Historical Society, and has held memberships in the Yamhill County Historical Society and the Oregon Historical Society. He is a life member of the OSU Alumni Association.

He is a Vietnam combat veteran and has lived in Newberg since 1993. With Lucy, he enjoys seven children and 15 grandchildren. ❖